Running Amok

Our Grandchildren will Curse Us!

DAVE ROSENAK

Trafford
PUBLISHING

Order this book online at www.trafford.com/08-0342
or email orders@trafford.com

Most Trafford titles are also available at major online book retailers.

Note for Librarians: A cataloguing record for this book is available from Library
and Archives Canada at www.collectionscanada.ca/amicus/index-e.html

ISBN: 978-1-4251-7357-9

*We at Trafford believe that it is the responsibility of us all, as both individuals
and corporations, to make choices that are environmentally and socially sound.
You, in turn, are supporting this responsible conduct each time you purchase a
Trafford book, or make use of our publishing services. To find out how you are
helping, please visit www.trafford.com/responsiblepublishing.html*

*Our mission is to efficiently provide the world's finest, most comprehensive
book publishing service, enabling every author to experience success.
To find out how to publish your book, your way, and have it available
worldwide, visit us online at www.trafford.com/10510*

 www.trafford.com

North America & international
toll-free: 1 888 232 4444 (USA & Canada)
phone: 250 383 6864 ♦ fax: 250 383 6804 ♦ email: info@trafford.com

The United Kingdom & Europe
phone: +44 (0)1865 722 113 ♦ local rate: 0845 230 9601
facsimile: +44 (0)1865 722 868 ♦ email: info.uk@trafford.com

10 9 8 7 6 5 4 3 2

FORWARD

Our forefathers "pledged their lives, their fortunes, and their sacred honor" in an extraordinary undertaking, knowing that if "they did not hang together, they would most assuredly hang separately". They did this "to secure the blessings of liberty for themselves and their posterity". What an amazing thing! They put their lives on the line to create opportunity for us, people who would be living more than two hundred years into the future!

And what are we doing today for our children, our grandchildren, and the generations to follow us?

We are overpopulating their world and burning up precious and irreplaceable resources, polluting the land, the water, and the air, and causing climate changes with likely disastrous consequences. We are destroying the forests and driving other species to extinction. We are promoting dogma over observation, reason and science, fostering intolerance for those different from ourselves, and deliberately squelching medical research that holds great promise. We continue to pursue failed policies with regards to narcotic drugs, immigration, and the Middle East. We continue to solve disputes with other nations with bombs and destruction, trade our freedom for a little perceived safety, detain people indefinitely without proof of wrongdoing, and we are discussing just how much we should torture those people! We are creating a nation that does not manufacture anything, provides enormous wealth for some and poverty for others, makes even basic health care inaccessible for millions, and we're building a mountain of debt for the next generation to repay!

We can do better!

So I sat down one day and made a list, and then expanded that list into this book, full of opinions for specific actions that I believe we as a society should be taking to improve life for ourselves and future generations.

It is said that opinions are like assholes:
Everybody has one.
Everybody thinks the other guy's stinks.

I don't expect that everyone will agree with all of my opinions.
I don't expect that anyone will agree with all of my opinions.
I expect that many people will want to tell me to take my stinking opinions and shove them back where the sun don't shine.

However, my purpose is not to convince everyone that my opinions are right.

It is that all people should have some well thought out and reasoned opinion on each of these subjects. If I can provoke thought and reflection, perhaps discussion and debate, and help cause people to think about these matters, then I will be satisfied that perhaps something worthwhile has been accomplished. I am not by any means an expert on any of the subjects discussed. I don't have the background, and haven't done the research. My main source of news is Jon Stewart, and turning for in depth analysis to Bill Maher. But perhaps this book may stimulate people who are experts on the various subjects discussed to put forth their recommendations, and to actually create solutions for some of the problems that confront us.

Certainly anyone running for public office should have carefully thought through each of these subjects and should have a clear and concise opinion as to what should be the approach of government toward them. It is a travesty that we can go through an election, and the electorate is not informed as to the thoughts of the candidates regarding subjects of great importance. You can not have a true democracy if the voters are forced to make their selections on nothing more than a candidate's good looks and sound bite commercials. The essence of democracy is a well informed electorate, able to make reasoned selection of candidates based on their qualifications and their positions on issues.

CONTENTS

CHAPTER 1
POPULATION

Our Grandchildren will curse us.

We have been endowed by the Creator with a great legacy. Planet Earth that is four and a half billion years old, with living things that have been evolving toward today for more than three and a half billion years. We ridicule the dinosaurs by referring to anything obsolete as a "dinosaur". However, the dinosaurs were able to rule the earth for 165 million years. Civilized humans have been on Planet Earth for only 10 thousand years, and we are well on our way toward destroying it. Overpopulation exacerbates all other problems. If we do not destroy the planet in some other manner sooner, we shall surely destroy it through overpopulation. Already, we are rapidly exhausting irreplaceable natural resources, destroying the rainforests, polluting the waterways and the atmosphere, and driving other species into extinction. World human population is currently growing at a pace to double every fifty years. From the current 6 billion people on the face of the planet to 12 billion fifty years from now, 24 billion one hundred years from now, and 48 billion in only one hundred fifty years. Though you and I will be dead in one hundred fifty years, in terms of geological time, one hundred fifty years is a blink. Can we really be that irresponsible?

There are, of course, "experts" who tell us that we do not need to worry about population growth. They point to a few countries such as The Czech Republic where populations are actually declining (but not to countries such as Afghanistan where the population is growing at a rate to double within the next 15 years!). They predict that the problem of rapidly escalating population will solve itself. That in fifty years human population will stop growing without any effort on our part to make that happen. But then, there are many "experts" who predict many things. How good was that weather forecast for last weekend? Did the can't-miss stock tip from your broker really double? Did the expert-pick win in the 6th race at Belmont? If these simple daily events are impossible to correctly predict, are there really "experts" who can reliably predict an unprecedented event fifty years into the future? Do we want to bet the future of the Planet on it?

Throughout history, and as recently as the generation of our grandparents, it was common in most cultures throughout the world and in the United States to have six, eight, a dozen, or more children. Populations were held in check because a large portion of the children died of complications at birth or of dread diseases before they reached maturity. Young women died giving birth. Having a multitude of children helped to soften the despair when some of them died.

Now we have developed the ability to eliminate most of the hideous diseases that have plagued mankind throughout the millennia, killing off children and young adults. At the same time, we have also developed the ability to avoid giving birth to mass quantities of children, and we don't even have to give up sex! It is the cruel law of nature that living things produce far more offspring than will survive. With most species, most of the offspring die as babies or while still young, from harsh conditions, disease, starvation, or by falling prey to predators, and that is what keeps populations stable. Humans have learned to overcome most of the causes of early death. But with our learning to survive comes the responsibility to control our desires for unrestrained reproduction. How can anyone profess a love for children, and yet doom them to live on an overcrowded overpopulated world?

In the United States, we continue to grow our population both through an excessive birth rate, and also by allowing our population to balloon by taking the overflow population from other parts of the world. The United States must become the proponent to the World for eliminating world population growth. We have tried to use our position as the most powerful nation on earth to champion other causes with the other nations on the planet, but we have utterly ignored this subject which is far and away the most important cause to the future of the planet. This is not a matter of meddling in the internal affairs of other nations. World population is not an internal affair. People migrate. Over time, the excess people born in one part of the world will end up in another. This is a world problem, and must be solved by the people of the world working on it together. And as the world leader, it falls upon the United States to spearhead a worldwide movement to eliminate the spiraling growth of human population.

To date, this is a topic utterly ignored by every politician in every office in the United States!

To take a stand on this issue will require some real backbone. It is a policy that will be reviled by most all religious groups. This seems surprising in that one would think that people devoted to God's works would certainly not want to destroy His planet. But yet, it is a basic tenet of nearly all religions: "Go Forth and Multiply". I don't know if this is just a carry-over from days gone by when it really was necessary to have large numbers of children to assure that there would be enough left after many died from pestilence, war, and famine, or if this is a deliberate power play plan to increase the numbers of your tribe and increase the importance of the leaders, or to increase the numbers of your tribe over the enemy tribe? But whatever the rationale, it is time to put it to rest. Religious leaders, particularly, should have the maturity to put aside slavery to tradition or desire for the power of increased numbers and work for the benefit of all mankind, for the benefit of the generations to follow, and for the benefit of God's Planet Earth.

Before we can preach population control to the world, we must adopt an internal policy to teach responsible parenting and to restrict family size. This needs to become a number one priority and a national goal. We are not talking great sacrifice here. It is not that no one will be allowed to have children, and that the sound of children laughing will never again be heard throughout the land. To have a stable population, we do need to give birth to and to raise to maturity an average of two children for every two adults. Many people, for a variety of reasons, have no children, or only one. Tragically, in spite of our tremendous gains in medical technology, some of our children still do not survive to maturity. So those who have the desire and ability to care for more could certainly have three or four. That's a bunch. It takes a lot of love, a lot of devotion, a lot of determination, and a lot of hard work to be good parents to three or four children. We simply need to resolve that that is enough.

Obviously, the first place to start with reducing birth rates is to adopt a policy of doing all possible to prevent unwanted pregnancies and unwanted births. We need to make family planning and sex education a part of the curriculum in every junior high school and every high school, at the ages where young people are first grappling with puberty. Before they reach the age where they begin sexual experimentation, young people must be taught that having children is not only the most rewarding experience they will ever undertake, it is also the most awesome responsibility they will ever assume. Raising children requires twenty years or more of intense commitment of time, effort, patience, and enormous amounts of money, and a lifetime commitment of love, devotion, and emotional support. It is an undertaking that should never be entered into by anyone who has not first established a stable and loving marital relationship, a stable career path, and full understanding and ardent desire for the task.

We need to make kids aware of contraceptive methods, and to encourage their use. We need to abandon a welfare system that has made child bearing a life choice for bored young teenage girls, a means of escaping a dreary life and setting up housekeeping at public expense. We need to scrap the "abstinence only" policy, and deal with the world as it really is. Yes, young kids should abstain from sex, but many of them won't. We need to arm them with thorough knowledge to deal with the physical and emotional complexities that are created by their journey to becoming adults.

It will be more difficult to get cooperation from other parts of the world, especially from countries where a culture of producing large numbers of progeny is deeply ingrained. Using whatever tools we have, the United States must engender the cooperation of the other nations of the Earth to join us in what is clearly the most vital requirement to preserve the planet Earth and the quality of life for its future human and non-human inhabitants. One of those tools, of course, would be that for any nation that refuses to adopt a "zero population growth" policy, the quota for their people to immigrate to the United States would become zero. The United States must become the champion for this cause, and educate, cajole, and coerce the world to participate.

Unfortunately, actual U.S. policy is the opposite. Since 1973, the United States has refused any foreign aid to be spent on abortions in any country that receives our aid. Then, in 1984, at a world population conference in Mexico City, Ronald Reagan instituted the "Mexico City Policy", also known as the "Global Gag Rule" that forbids any U.S. aid to any clinic anywhere that even discusses abortion. Although that was rescinded by President Clinton, it was reinstated immediately upon the ascendancy of George W. Bush, with the further dictate that clinics that receive U.S. aid must preach "Abstinence Only" as the only means of contraception. This has forced the closure of thousands of clinics in poor rural areas in Eastern Europe, in Asia, and in Africa, where those clinics were the only resources to provide contraception, sex education, prenatal and obstetric care. According to the Guttmacher Institute, a non-profit organization focused on sexual and reproductive issues, worldwide there are some forty-six million abortions performed, and nineteen million of those are performed by untrained people using improper methods under unsafe conditions, resulting in serious long term health problems or death for more than five million women a year. By making condoms difficult to obtain in poor regions of the world, we have actually dramatically increased the number of abortions! And, we have promoted the spread of disease. Not only are we not the champion for promoting reproductive health and reasonable reproductive choices in the world, we are among the greatest impediments for that cause. (Sara Paretsky, Chicago Tribune, 1/7/07)

If we are able to eliminate population growth, there will be some real and serious side affects. Our economy is based on having continual expansion in all areas of business, continual expansion of building and construction, and, an ever-growing number of young people to support a growing population of old people. Learning how to cope without this growing population will be a real challenge. But if we do not face that challenge now, do we really want to pass the task on to our children and our children's children, when the number of humans on Earth is even greater, and the task is even more difficult? If eliminating the growth of population creates severe economic problems, would the problems of actually trying to contract an overgrown population not be that much more daunting?

CHAPTER 2
PETROLEUM

Another legacy issue. In four and a half billion years, the planet has created large pools of liquid petroleum in various spots under the surface of the Earth. The petroleum has been created from decaying vegetation in a process requiring millions of years.

We are planning to use it all up in the next few decades!

There is some argument over exactly how much there is, and how long we can keep finding it faster than we use it up, but it is only a question of a decade or two. And as a billion people in China and a billion people in India come to want their share, we will be using it up faster and faster.

In addition to robbing this valuable resource from our children and grandchildren, we are well aware that burning petroleum emits pollutants that are destroying the Earth's atmosphere, and causing climate change of unknown, but likely disastrous, consequences.

As the demand continues to outstrip the supply, we continue to transfer vast power and vast sums of money to those who control the remaining quantities. This creates extraordinarily rich tyrants and despots in various countries of the Middle East, South America, Africa, and elsewhere. Most of these abuse their own populations, and deflect the misery of their people by blaming their poor condition on the outside world, particularly the United States. This has destabilized the world, and created a nightmare for all of us.

We were whacked between the eyes with this problem more than thirty year ago when OPEC first got together and suddenly quadrupled the price of oil, creating economic chaos for us. A few years later, we where whacked again when the Ayatollah took over in Iran, and they doubled the price of oil again. All these years later, we have done nothing about it.

After the attacks of September 11, 2001 wasn't it clear that the first step that should have been taken was to adopt emergency plans to radically reduce petroleum use. And isn't it clear that in trying to deal with the abusive governments of the Middle East we have radically reduced options because they, so to speak, have us "over a barrel"? If we were "at war", an obvious step would have been to implement rationing, as we have in previous wars. Before someone says "but the United States does not import much oil from the Middle East", surely we all realize that oil is a fungible commodity. Whether the oil from the Middle East comes here or elsewhere the effect is the same. The world supply of oil is in an incredibly delicate balance, with the world consumption virtually equal to the current potential for the world to supply it. Regardless of where the specific barrels of oil we use come from, if we continue to consume at the level we currently do, we will continue to drive the price of oil up, and continue to create an enormous windfall of money for those who wish to destroy us. And yet, after the attacks of 9/11, the subject of dealing with oil dependence wasn't even broached. We certainly recognized that money was a major weapon in the "War on Terror". We went after bank accounts of suspected terrorist organizations. We shut down organizations claiming to be raising money for charity if we suspected that they were funneling money to terrorist organizations. But we ignored the elephant in the room. If we want to know who it is that is financing terrorists, the obvious answer is: "it is us". We are sending hundreds of billions of dollars into the hands of every evil despot who has the good fortune not only to have oil under his feet but also to have an incredibly stupid adversary in the United States

Yes, over a period of years, the supply of oil might be increased, or alternative fuels could come into production, but in the near term the situation is precarious. When a hurricane blows in the Gulf, when Russia shuts down some production to punish the people running Yukos, or oil workers in Nigeria go on strike, or Hugo Chavez has a mood swing, chaos reigns. Avoiding any interruption in the oil supply is a primary consideration in any policy regarding tyrants in oil producing regions. For instance, in weighing our options of dealing with Iran, first and foremost, is the consideration that they could not only withhold their oil, but that they could shut down shipping oil from the entire Middle East through the Straits of Hormuz. The world would experience economic collapse.

No one knows just what technology will replace petroleum fuel, but necessity is the mother of invention. We should have started artificially increasing the cost of petroleum fuel through a gradual implementation of add-on taxes thirty year ago to the point that we would conserve and we would look for alternatives, and alternatives would become economically viable. And in fact, the added taxes may only reflect the actual cost of petroleum, factoring in the military costs of dealing with the monsters we have created, and the costs of periodic disruptions to our economy any time there is any disruption to the petroleum supply.

Petroleum has been cheap: Cost of pumping it from liquid pools under the ground – a few dollars a barrel. Cost of refining it – a few dollars more. Cost after we use it all up – Priceless!

With the added taxes, gasoline today might cost six or eight or more dollars a gallon, but the beauty of raising the price through taxes is that the money goes right back into our own pocket – not to greedy oil tycoons or evil despots. The revenues produced can simply allow us to reduce other taxes elsewhere. Also, you the consumer might not even spend any more for gasoline than you do now. If you pay two to three times as much per gallon but use one half or one third as much per mile, your total outlay for gasoline might be the same. Look at the Europeans, who have high priced fuels, driving their Smart Cars and riding on their Vespas. And they are developing radical technology like the French car that runs on compressed air!

By creating a predictable increase in the cost of fuel years into the future, much of the good that can be accomplished by this slow steady increase in add-on taxes will occur long before the actual increases even take place. When you buy the new car, if you know that gasoline prices will increase 50% over the next five years that you intend to keep it, it will certainly influence your buying decision. Not only will you know how your cost of operating the car will be increasing, but you can also consider: will there be any re-sale market for a gas-guzzler five years from now? Certainly, the people designing cars, in addition to the people making decisions regarding tooling and facilities for cars that will be built three to five years from now, will be able to predict and take into consideration what effects the increasing costs of fuel will have on the desires and demands of the public. If you are running an oil fueled furnace in your house, factory, or commercial building, knowing what the costs of heating oil will be years down the road will enable you to better calculate the pay-back from a conversion to a more efficient furnace, or to a different fuel, or to electric heating, or to adding solar panels. If you are running an oil company, you will know that you had better start putting a lot more emphasis and money into R&D for the next generation of fuels.

Of course, the taxes would be adjusted for fuel containing ethanol, bio-diesel, or other non-petroleum elements. The taxes would also be adjusted to compensate for higher cost petroleum – derived from oil shale, tar sands, or other non-traditional sources. This would equalize the higher cost of these fuels, make them economically viable, and encourage their production and use.

And the added cost of fuel would certainly make trucking companies more aware of maximizing their fuel efficiencies. It would give a big boost to a preference for buying merchandise from local suppliers, and minimizing the need for shipping. It might tip the balance in favor of more shipping by rail or by boat. Who knows what innovations in commercial transportation might result if there were sufficient incentive to seek them? This morning's Chicago Tribune carried an article about engineers from the Illinois Institute of Technology developing a very affordable kit to convert diesel trucks and busses to hybrids. Their research showed that the busses could get double the miles per gallon and emit half the pollutants.

For a little while, when gasoline prices first spiked over $3 per gallon, automobile ads began to feature fuel efficiency numbers. Those numbers have virtually disappeared from the ads again. Does no one care? Or do the automobile makers and sellers not care? Is fuel efficiency just not sexy? They would rather feature gargantuan vehicles climbing mountains and crossing streams? How high do we need to raise the price of fuel until the public will care? And when the buying public cares, the ads will again feature fuel efficiency numbers, and the manufacturers will be in a race to see who can offer the most attractive vehicle with the most attractive fuel efficiency. It isn't that I don't prefer to drive a big SUV. But we are all spoiled rotten and perpetuating a myth that we can do anything we want, drive the biggest most inefficient vehicle we want. The phrase "We are Addicted to Oil" is nonsense! We have no craving for oil; we have an utter disregard for oil! What we are addicted to is satisfying our every whim without regard to the consequences. If we make the monster car unaffordable, we will adjust! We do adjust our expectations and even our desires to economic reality all the time. I might actually prefer to have my chauffer to be driving me around in my Rolls Royce, but I have never felt deprived because I don't have a chauffer, nor a Rolls

Royce. We will adjust, we will get used to driving smaller more efficient vehicles, and maybe we will all feel better about ourselves knowing that we have not robbed a precious resource from our children and despoiled their planet.

And we're not really talking sacrifice here. My Pontiac Vibe is a bargain priced four door five passenger vehicle that is built like an SUV – put the bike rack on the back, the canoe on top, or fold the seats down and there is plenty of room to load in a stack of eight foot long lumber - and it gets over 30 miles to the gallon. The Ford Escape Hybrid is an SUV that gets 36 miles per gallon. The Toyota Prius Hybrid is a four door five passenger sedan with all the luxury features, and it gets up to 60 miles per gallon. If the technology for fuel efficient cars exists right now, today, why aren't all the manufacturers adapting it to all their passenger vehicles?

I pulled up alongside a humongous new SUV the other day, and checked the web site to see if it was really as big as it seemed. Yep! Three tons of shiny black steel and chrome, 18 feet long, 6 feet high, 6 ½ feet wide, with 400 surging horses under the hood. Boy does that validate your manhood! Driving around town it gets 13 miles to the gallon.

If we want to make a dramatic improvement in the twin problems of scarce petroleum and atmospheric pollution from burning petroleum in the next few years, there is no other way to do it than to replace the American fleet with cars that are available today and that burn vastly less petroleum fuel per mile. Talking about changing our driving habits, biking to work, walking to the corner store, or even riding public transportation - all are good things to do. But none of them are going to put a dent in the amount of gasoline we burn. And waiting for new technology – who knows for how long? And as new technology is developed, we still have the years required to replace the cars currently on the road before we will substantially reduce petroleum usage.

One concept that has not been discussed is the development of a small inexpensive car specifically intended for commuting, powered by batteries with seats for two people, no cargo, and a seventy mile range. Commuting and short drives around town account for up to 90% of most people's driving. A family with two drivers/workers might have two commuter cars (that together fit in one space in the garage where they recharge overnight), and one family car that sits in the other space to be used for the 10% of the time that it is really needed. Businesses could put metered recharging stations in their parking lots, and downtown parking lots could add recharging stations as well. There could be metered recharging stations along the curb in city residential neighborhoods for those who park on the street overnight. People could drive their electric commuter car most of the time, and if they don't own one, rent a larger gasoline powered vehicle for an occasional road trip or other event that required it.

But no one in Congress has dared mention "higher taxes" to create "higher priced gasoline and heating oil". The concept that it, in fact, would just be a trade-off and not really cost anyone anything seemed too complicated to try to explain to the public, too much risk of turning off voters. So instead of doing the right thing, they did what they always do - they added more regulations, and added more giveaways. They passed CAFE standards - the Corporate Average Fuel Economy act. It attempts to require that manufacturers produce vehicles with increasing average fuel efficiency across all the vehicles they produce. Ultimately, though, the manufacturers must produce the vehicles that consumers want to buy. CAFE standards do nothing to change the preferences of consumers. During the time they have been in effect, we have seen the advent of bigger, heavier, and more inefficient SUVs – vehicles designed to carry eight or nine passengers while driving through fields and streams and up mountains. Activities for which they are never used. Prior to implementing CAFE standards, there were almost no SUVs, Conversion Vans or Pick-up Trucks with luxury four door cabs, all of which are "Light Trucks", and now comprise a substantial portion of our passenger carrying fleet. Of course, CAFE standards were made to allow "Light Trucks" to be much more inefficient than "Passenger Vehicles". And although passenger cars have become somewhat more efficient, with the advent of the "Light Trucks" replacing a large portion of the "Passenger Vehicles" the average miles-per-gallon of U.S. vehicles has scarcely improved at all. CAFE standards do nothing to promote car pooling, use of public transportation, moving closer to the work place, or any other means of reducing the amounts of fuel used. And, of course, CAFE standards do nothing to promote the development of alternative fuels or energy sources. And as ineffective as they are, the U.S. Auto Manufacturers are busy lobbying Congress for looser standards. Do they not see the handwriting so clearly emblazoned on the wall? With the U.S. Auto Manufacturers rapidly losing market share and going broke, can't they see that continuing to try to prop up a market for monster cars isn't working?

The other method for Congress to deal with the problem is to pass energy bills with giveaways. Giveaways that actually do cost you and me – they are giving away our money. And there is no evidence for the assumption that Congress either knows where best to give it, or that they even make their decisions on that basis. Congress is motivated by what sounds good, and what will produce more campaign contributions, and more votes, not on what will best solve real problems. Giving money to Midwest corn farmers sounds great and plays well in a campaign. Giving money to Archer Daniels Midland to build more ethanol plants elicits great campaign contributions. But the viability of ethanol from corn as an automotive fuel is highly suspect. There is considerable evidence that producing corn ethanol requires burning more fuel than it produces. That when all the pollutants created in the process of growing, harvesting, and converting corn to ethanol fuel are taken into account, that the amount of pollutants dumped into the atmosphere is greater than if we burned gasoline. Also, it is estimated that to produce enough corn to satisfy all our energy needs would require a land area several times that of the United States.

Sugar is a vastly better crop for producing ethanol than corn, and inherently produces ethanol at a cost at least 25% below the cost of producing ethanol from corn. Ironically, as short sighted as we have been, it is fascinating to note that Brazil foresaw the coming problem decades ago, at a time when their supply of petroleum fuel was still plentiful and cheap. They began planting millions of acres of sugar cane, developing improved methods for using it to produce ethanol fuel, and building refineries to do so. They heavily subsidized this activity for all these years and some said they were crazy. But who has the last laugh now, when they are completely energy independent, with an entire fleet of nonpolluting cars.

And in fact, Brazil has enough farmland to triple the 4.6 billion gallons of ethanol per year they are currently making, and could increase their production to be able to supply enough ethanol to replace 5% of the oil consumed worldwide. (Chicago Tribune 3/14/07). But our Congress has, of course, enacted a protective tariff making it impractical for us to buy ethanol from Brazil. It also has enacted protective tariffs to protect us from imported sugar, which is rapidly driving all of the candy manufacturers out of the United States. And are we doing anything to dramatically expand sugar production in the U.S, and develop a sugar based ethanol industry? Or would that upset the corn farmer's lobby? How much acreage is there in the U.S that would be suitable to growing sugar? Could we promote joint ventures with Mexico, Central American nations, and Caribbean Island nations to vastly expand sugar farming, and build plants for the production of sugar based ethanol? And, at the same time, provide an enormous economic boost to some nations that could surely use it? And, perhaps, reduce the incentive for people from those nations to add to our problems with a flood of immigrants? Is anything being done along these lines?

As it happens, the relation between supply and demand of petroleum does come and go over the years. From time to time the price of petroleum fuels soars, and we all become very concerned, vowing to "do something". We pledge that our next car will be fuel efficient. We wring our hands and talk about the need to develop alternative fuels. In the 70's, after the first "oil crises" investors poured millions of dollars into developing the extraction of the oil from the oil shale in the Rockies. But then, there will be a period where oil suddenly seems plentiful. There is, in fact, very little storage capacity, so if supply temporarily exceeds usage even by a little, suddenly there appears to be a glut of oil. In the late 90's, briefly, the price of oil dropped under $10 per barrel, and a gallon of gasoline sold retail for under $1.00. We promptly forgot all about an "energy problem". The investors in Rocky Mountain shale oil lost their millions. And investors are reluctant to pour money again into such fickle long term ventures.

No, our government trying to regulate and trying to select the technologies to back with giveaways is not the answer. Ultimately, the market price of petroleum fuels will permanently rise to the point that the market will force solutions - some combination of conservation, public transportation, alternate fuels, lifestyle changes, or other as yet unforeseen innovations. But we could speed that process up, avoid depriving our children of a valuable resource, avoid despoiling their planet, and avoid giving away trillions of dollars to the oil cartel and the oil tycoons.

Anyone who has been in Congress over the past three decades that we have been so acutely aware of this impending disaster and done nothing about it should be ashamed of themselves.

CHAPTER 3
BALANCED BUDGET

And yet another legacy issue.

What is a "Budget" if it doesn't balance expected expenses with expected revenue? That is the definition of a budget! The whole purpose is to balance. Otherwise, if you're just going to spend without regard to income, why bother with a budget? How can anyone in the United States Congress look at himself or herself in the mirror after passing a "Budget" with a planned deficit of hundreds of Billions of dollars which add to previous deficits they have enacted, further amplifying a humongous national debt exceeding nine Trillion dollars?

There are a tremendous number of Americans who are extraordinarily wealthy. Everywhere you look, small houses are being knocked down, and mansions being built. Resort areas around the country are ballooning with million dollar "second homes" – mansions that nobody even lives in for most of the year. Autos selling for fifty thousand dollars are considered "normal", not extravagant. Now there is nothing wrong with being rich, but it is criminal that at the same time we are lavishing luxury upon ourselves, we are piling up debts as a burden upon our children and grandchildren.

And although some of those very wealthy people got that way through hard work, invention, and innovation, others simply had the good fortune to be born to the right parents, and their wealth is what is left of an inheritance after they have done their best to blow it. Others have accumulated great wealth by getting lucky – winning the lottery, or having great success as movie stars, TV stars, rock stars, or star athletes. Others have accumulated their wealth by finding someone with deep pockets to sue, or finding lots of clients and suing lots of people. Regardless of how they have managed to latch on to their wealth, they are equally protective of keeping it all for themselves. "I earned it, and it's mine." But isn't the ability to earn great wealth, to a large extent, a product of living in America? Haven't those people reaped an inordinate benefit from the American way of life? Hasn't the contribution and sacrifice of all who have gone before created a system that allows people to make vast wealth? And don't those who have so richly reaped the benefits owe a debt to society and to future generations to carry the burden to provide for the needs of Government, and to not burden those future generations with our debt?

I had a conversation a while ago with a wealthy friend in which I brought up the need to provide for the children of the next generation. I don't know if he truly didn't understand the question, but his answer, I am afraid, was typical: "I have provided for my children's future".

It isn't that the concept of the wealthy carrying the burden is new. In the past, we have had a graduated income tax with much higher rates for those at the upper end of earnings. From WW II until 1964, the top rate was 91%, and then reduced to 70% until 1981, when it was reduced to 50%. And Capital Gains, which are the favorite vehicle for the very wealthy to get wealthier, have not always been taxed at rates lower than the income people earn by working for it. Income from investments already receives favored treatment over earned income because it is not subject to the 15.3%

taxes for FICA and Medicare. I don't suggest a return to a confiscatory 91% tax on income – it is counter productive and forces people to find ways to work around the system, to take benefits that do not show up as taxable income, and acts as a disincentive to productive effort. But greed and power, and powerful greedy people, have devolved to the current system where the wealthy pay little in taxes, we do not pay for what we spend, and we continue to run up ever larger debts.

And, of course, nobody really knows how much debt we can accumulate before it causes economic collapse. If Joe Doakes habitually spends more than his income, as long as he makes the minimum payments on his credit cards each month, there is no sign of a problem. The credit card companies consider Joe to be a great customer. They send him letters praising him and send him more and more cards, and extend to him higher and higher credit limits. He is living the life of a fat cat. This may go on for many years. There are stories of people with modest incomes running up credit card debt of hundreds of thousands of dollars. Until some day, suddenly, unexpectedly, and without warning, some credit manager realizes that Joe has far too much debt, cuts him off, and refuses to extend more credit. Joe is in trouble, and he never saw it coming! Joe is unable to make his payments, and they reposes his Cadillac and his big screen TV, foreclose on the house, his wife leaves him, and he is pushing his belongings down the street in a shopping cart! Does anyone really know how far in debt the United States of America can go before the world cuts us off, and we're all pushing our belongings in a shopping cart?

Of course, we are financing our government fiscal debt, to a large extent, by continuously incurring an enormous trade debt. We import billions of dollars of merchandise, and send the people in the foreign nations supplying that merchandise U.S. Dollars. But we do not produce any merchandise that they want to buy at the prices we want to sell it. So they are stuck with U.S. Dollars and have nothing to do with them other than to buy our Government debt, Treasury Bills, Notes and Bonds. Of course, they can spend some of the dollars to buy our cities, and to buy our corporations, but they still hold two trillion dollars of our Government debt. What happens when the Chinese, the Japanese, or the countries of OPEC decide to seek higher returns and begin to dump their U.S. Treasury Securities? We recently had a panic in the financial markets at the mere mention by a Chinese official that they were considering doing so.

In the meantime, we are reducing tax rates for incredibly rich people, and eliminating the tax on capital gains which only pile up as a result of being rich. We are even talking about eliminating taxes on rich dead people. If anybody can afford to pay taxes without it being a burden on their life style, it would certainly be rich dead people!

I don't like to pay taxes. Nobody likes to pay taxes. But when we talk about "tax relief", doesn't that imply that we have reduced spending and are able to reduce taxes because less money is needed? If all we are doing is not paying our bills, how is that "tax relief"? What a great plan! I can get richer if I don't pay my bills! Is the theory that no one will ever have to pay for what we spend today? We'll just keep putting it on the credit card forever? Or have we just pushed the date that we need to pay a little further down the road, but with added interest, and we'll all be dead by then anyway and it can be a problem for our kids?

CHAPTER 4
GOVERNMENT

"We hold these truths to be self-evident, that all men are created equal, that they are endowed by their Creator with certain unalienable Rights, that among these are Life, Liberty and the pursuit of Happiness. That to secure these rights, Governments are instituted among Men, deriving their just powers from the consent of the governed."

"We the People of the United States, in Order to form a more perfect Union, establish Justice, insure domestic Tranquility, provide for the common defense, promote the general Welfare, and secure the Blessings of Liberty to ourselves and our Posterity, do ordain and establish this Constitution for the United States of America."

The rights of people are endowed by the Creator, not by the government. Nowhere does it say that the purpose of government is to tell us what is morally right or wrong. The government that does that is the Taliban! The Taliban that makes it a crime to sing or to dance. The Taliban with a horde of morality police to beat women who leave the house without a male escort, or who allow an ankle to show. The Taliban who would stone to death a suspected adulteress. Is that what we want? A government run by people with such certitude that they will decide for all of us what is and what is not moral, what is and what is not acceptable or desirable behavior?

The President, Senators, and all the other people in our government work for us, and it is important that we and they understand that. The President should address you with the respect due his employer, and not vice versa. And you can pat him on the back and tell him what a fine job he is doing.

How did we start elevating these people to royalty? It may not seem to matter much, addressing people as The Right Honorable Senator........, or standing when Mister President ..... enters the room, but does it set the wrong tone? Do we forget who works for whom? Do we encourage the people that we elect to do a job for us to consider themselves to have rank and privilege? Is this how they have come to believe that empowering and enriching themselves and their cronies is the purpose of their job?

We have further corrupted the process by expecting that our Senators and Representatives will pander to us, and to our local pet projects, and not to the greater good of the Nation. Was it originally intended that a "Representative" was primarily to promote local interests? Is the system of earmarks, money for pet local projects determined not by merit, but by the rank and power of the member of Congress who proposes it, what we really want? And if all the Senators and Representatives are busy lobbying for local interests, who is looking out for National interests, and the interests of the people of Planet Earth? Has Congress actually created any significant or groundbreaking legislation since the Civil Rights Acts of the 1960s? (And they were pushed into that by the Court.) And if Congressmen are tying earmarks for local interests into major appropriations and other legislation, are they then voting for those bills because they really believe that they have merit, or because their earmark is tied to it? And are they horse-trading with other members of Congress – you vote for the bill with my earmark, and I'll vote for yours?

Five hundred people in Congress are way too many. The concept of a two chamber legislature goes back to ancient England where it was a compromise between the nobility and the commoners – a distinction we presumably have done away with. Our own Congress was a compromise between more populous states and those who felt that their interests would be overwhelmed due to their smaller populations. The real purpose today is to see to it that major issues are never addressed nor resolved. We have enormous waste with five hundred Senators and Representatives, each with a sizeable staff, and each creating boondoggles and pet projects for the folks back home so they will get re-elected. Most people don't know who their Senators and Representatives are, nor do they know what they do. Congress should be reconfigured to a single chamber with about twenty five members, each elected from a region of the nation. There would be a New England Congressperson, a Mid-Atlantic Congressperson, etc. Few enough that each will recognize that the responsibility for action rests squarely on their own shoulders. That their vote is not just one of hundreds on a bill that will be sent to the other chamber to be revised before it has any chance of being implemented. And few enough that we can pay attention to who they are and what they accomplish, and actually hold them accountable for what they do, or fail to do. The concept of concentrating power in a smaller group sounds scary. But in fact, over the past sixty years, most of the major improvements in making our society one that embraces the rights and dignity of all its members and that allows freedom of choice in such major decisions as whether or not to have a child, have come from a group of just nine people. And that group is not elected; they are appointed for life, and are not even responsive to the pressure of needing to stand for reelection. And look at the enormous economic power we have placed in the few individuals who run the Federal Reserve, another group that is not elected.

If Congresspersons are not representing small local areas, there will be far less incentive to act as a local politician, and to begin to act as a Congressperson for the Nation as a whole. We should retain the concept of replacing a portion of them every couple years. It will keep them responsive to the desires of the citizens. It will avoid a particular group or philosophy from becoming so entrenched that it can no longer be dislodged.

But if there are only twenty five people in Congress, who will comprise committees to investigate subjects and make recommendations to the Congress? That would be turned over to professionals in the field being investigated, people who actually have background, knowledge, and insight into the subject being reviewed. If Congress is trying to pass legislation for an energy policy, rather than having a committee of Congressmen, who are total amateurs in the subject, investigate and recommend, the committee would be comprised of scientists and executives with vast knowledge and understanding of the subject. Matters of budget would be investigated by a committee of bankers, economists, and accounting executives. A committee to investigate why health care costs have exploded, and how to get them under control, and how to provide universal health care, would be comprised of doctors, hospital administrators, and health insurance professionals, people who actually might understand the subject and might have useful proposals to deal with it. Lord knows the current system has produced no meaningful energy policy at all, and a budget that is bloated and projects enormous deficits, and a disaster of a health care system.

The Congresspersons then might have to actually read the recommendations of the committees, listen to discussions of the topics, and make informed judgments. They might even read the bills they vote on before they vote on them! Congress might not have time to spend weeks debating a new name for fried potatoes (Freedom Fries) or months occupied discussing an impeachment for a blow job. They might not spend months debating whether some U.S. Attorneys were dismissed for political reasons – of course they were. They might have to skip the enormous heart wrenching debates over passing "non-binding" resolutions. One of my favorite lines is from the play/movie "1776" when the

Continental Congress is supposed to be debating a resolution to declare independence from Great Britain: "Piddle, twiddle, and resolve, not one damn thing do we solve". Perhaps we could do away with the pomp, the ceremony, the grandstanding, with such incredibly arcane and sophomoric practices as the filibuster, and get down to the business of running and improving the Nation.

It is widely assumed that winning elections is about raising money. I'm not sure why – political ads generally contain no useful information whatsoever, and generally boil down to just telling us that their opponent is a douche bag. Does anyone really pay any attention? Do we really care how many places the candidates have visited, or how many VFW chapters they have addressed? Perhaps in a society that considers watching people on television eat bugs and vote each other off the island, these sound bites really are what swings elections. Will we vote for the "Uniter not Divider" no mater how many wedge issues he seizes on to fracture the country into "Red People" and "Blue People", and fracture the world into those who are "With Us" and those who are "Agin' Us"?

Surely the money does corrupt. The politicians do become beholden to those supplying the money. And the waste of time and resources pursuing money certainly gets in the way of doing their jobs. And the voters have nothing but sound bites on which to base their votes. And the rich and powerful do get elected, regardless of whether that serves the interests of those who elected them.

Better by far, would be to totally prohibit the use of private or public funds in campaigning, and to utterly prohibit all political advertisements. And to replace the current system with a system where candidates would prepare a position paper spelling out their qualifications, and what they intend to accomplish if elected. Candidates for all offices would also take part in debates with their opponents, which would be aired on radio and television, and recorded on CDs. These position papers and CDs would be mailed to all eligible voters and posted on the internet a couple months prior to the election. All of this would be at public expense. It might be the best investment we could ever make. We might actually learn a little about the people for whom we are voting, and they might actually be looking to serve our interests. And without the political ads, we'll just have to rely on the news media to tell us which of our elected officials are douche bags.

This is not to say that their opinion on an issue will never change. In the last few years, particularly, there has been a great deal of rhetoric extolling the idea that it is a virtue for a politician to never change his or her position on an issue. In the last presidential election, much was made of John Kerry "flipping and flopping" on the issues (although I thought they were actually being kind to him, I was never able to discern that he had any positions on any issues). But, just where does the line cross from well reasoned conviction to being stubborn and pig headed?

Every day we all, of necessity, make decisions based on the information we can obtain, which is always incomplete. A condensed version of this happens in a card game. You can see the cards you were dealt, and you can draw inferences from the bidding or betting as to the cards others hold. Based on the limited information available, you are forced to form opinions as to the lie of the unseen cards, and develop a plan of action. As the play progresses, you see additional action and additional cards, and only a fool would not adjust his opinion as to the unseen cards, and adjust his plan of action. Of course, after the hand is over, someone is sure to pipe up and tell you how you misanalyzed the situation, and screwed up. And after a few moments thought, you may have to admit that they are right.

So it is with life. We work with the information we have, make reasoned judgments about the information we don't have, and make projections about events yet to come. From this we form opinions and develop plans of action. When possible, we avoid or delay irreversible commitment, and, keeping options open, seek to obtain additional information and additional insight. As the future unfolds, we find where we may have been wrong about existing facts, or mistaken in our projections, and we adjust our plan of action. In hindsight, we see the mistakes in facts, and the mistakes in analysis of those facts. If we do not see them, certainly we will be blessed with someone else who will be only too happy to point them out for us.

We would hope that people running our Government would make decisions, particularly important decisions, based on complete knowledge and perfect analysis. But it isn't so. Being a "Flip-Flopper" is not necessarily the worst thing that you can call a person.

And isn't it time we do away with the incredibly arcane and convoluted method of electing a President? Not only do we have an Electoral College getting in the way of allowing the majority of the voters being able to choose their President, but we also have this mystifying collection of primaries and caucuses in each state, with different dates and different rules for each. By the time we get to the election, we will have had two years of people who are supposed to be doing their jobs as Senators or Governors, instead participating in a traveling circus on display in every village school house or Moose hall, followed by the gaudy shows of the National Conventions. And when we finally get to the election, we can have third party candidates on the ballot siphoning votes from one of the candidates, which could enable another candidate to be elected even though the majority of the voters strongly disapprove of them. Wouldn't it be better by far to have a National Primary six months before the election to whittle the initial field of Presidential aspirants to five or six who actually have some chance of being elected. And then another primary three months before the election to bring the choice down to just two candidates, so that no one can be elected without the support of the majority of the voters.

CHAPTER 5
CRIME & PUNISHMENT

The object of criminal law, the courts, and the penal system should be to protect us from criminals. Particularly violent criminals. Under the current system, very few criminals, even violent ones, ever actually go to trial. The plea bargain system has evolved because it allows both prosecutor and defense attorneys to claim an easy victory, and unclogs crowded court schedules. Unfortunately not only doesn't it deal with the problem, but it intensifies it. We take violent, antisocial people and lock them away with other violent, antisocial people for a year or two. We place them in a situation where they are brutalized by the biggest strongest meanest inmates, and then we release them back into society meaner and nastier than when they went in. When released, they have the stigma of a criminal record, giving them few if any choices for legitimate employment. They remain free until they are caught committing mayhem against new victims. Or worse, they wear the prison record as a badge of honor before impressionable young people and become leaders of gangs, corrupting and creating more violent young criminals.

Also, the plea bargain system smacks of the inquisition. Confess your crimes and it will go easier on you. The plea bargain system is not designed to determine whether the accused is actually guilty of a crime, but only whether he can be coerced into accepting the proposed sentence. Anyone faced with a choice of a potential lifetime in prison, or one year in prison with six months off for good behavior, might well opt for the plea bargain, utterly without regard to his or her actual guilt or innocence.

Part of the problem with actually trying the accused is the horribly complex and time consuming trial procedure. Just selecting a jury can take days. Playing to jurors makes a circus out of the trial. Also, being on jury duty is disruptive to people's lives. Jurors should be professionals, trained and qualified for their ability to process evidence and reach intelligent and unbiased conclusions. There should be schools for teaching the art of serving on a jury, how to listen to testimony, separate the relevant from the irrelevant, take notes, and arrive at reasonable conclusions based on the evidence presented. We might be able to get away from gimmickry – "If the glove don't fit, you must acquit". This could be a wonderful second career for people who have retired from their original career, have decades of experience dealing with life and with people, and have maturity of judgment. After completing a training course, prospective jurors would be required to take qualifying exams where they would watch and listen to filmed testimony and be tested on their ability to reach reasonable, logical, and unbiased conclusions. They would go through mock jury deliberations, debate their view of the evidence with others, and be evaluated for their ability to present their views and to listen to the views of others.

As for "a jury of one's peers", in our society aren't we all "peers"? Is a group of people well trained and well qualified any less "peers"? Is there any reason to believe that a group of people deliberately selected by lawyers because they are biased to the lawyer's cause any better?

After creating a large pool of truly qualified jurors, the jury for a trial would be selected at random from those available. A jury would show up at the date and time for which the trial is scheduled, ready to proceed with presentation of the evidence.

The exclusion of "tainted" evidence, exclusion of "hearsay" evidence, and exclusion of a history of previous arrests and convictions and other tools for managing the information available to the jury should be eliminated. If a jury is intelligent enough to judge guilt or innocence, certainly they are capable of lending proper weight to the reliability of evidence. Surely jury members are capable of understanding that hearsay evidence related by a witness that did not actually see or hear the events being described is less reliable than evidence related by the person claiming to have directly observed it. Yes, there is an additional person who may be lying. And yes, there may be misunderstanding between the direct witness and the one retelling it. And if the direct witness is not present, they can not be cross examined. But that does not mean that hearsay evidence is necessarily bogus, or of no value. If police have obtained evidence through illegal search and seizure, those policemen should be disciplined – however if the evidence exists, it should be presented to the jury. This is not a game. It is a life and death matter, not only for the accused, but also for the future victims of a violent criminal who is released to continue to prey upon society. The concept that "better a thousand guilty men go free than that one innocent man is wrongly convicted" certainly sounds noble. But when considered from the point of view of all the innocent victims of people who were wrongly released to commit additional acts of mayhem, there is nothing reasonable and nothing noble about it. The ideal is that the legal system would be infallible, always perfectly discerning the guilty from the innocent. But reality is that that is an ideal that should certainly be strived for, but that will not be perfectly attained. And to the extent that there will be errors, there is risk involved with errors in either direction: risk of imprisoning an innocent man; risk of freeing a menace to society who will cause untold misery to a multitude of future victims.

Once a jury has determined beyond a reasonable doubt that a person accused of committing acts of violence against his fellow man is, in fact, guilty, the violent criminal needs to be permanently removed from society. The popular "three strikes laws" make no sense at all – why would you tell a violent criminal to go commit mayhem against more innocent victims until he is caught two more times? There are, of course, stories of ex-convicts who have gone straight and been model citizens. Unfortunately, there are far more stories of ex-convicts robbing, raping, maiming, and killing multiple victims. And for each direct victim, there are a number of indirect victims - husbands, wives, mothers, fathers, children, and all the other people around the victim's life who also suffer the trauma of having a family member or friend who has been attacked, raped, maimed, or murdered. It is common practice to offer grief counseling to an entire student body when one of their classmates has been brutally murdered. There is a dread that permeates the entire community with the knowledge that they are not so safe as they had hoped. No one has yet shown a method of dealing with violent criminals that doesn't have horrible rates of recidivism. We must be more concerned with the welfare of the future victims than with the welfare of the criminal.

Prisons should be built to house violent criminals as humanely as possible, but at minimum cost. And that may mean that they do not have visitors, and do not mix with each other. Having violent prisoners mixing with each other requires vastly more guards, and a facility that is substantially more complicated in order to create the secure spaces for the prison population to congregate. It constitutes cruel and unusual punishment for the weaker of the prisoners who will be brutalized by the stronger. Having violent men congregating also produces the likelihood of riots, and danger to the guards. It also lends added possibility of corruption of the guards, who may be subjected through bribes and/or threats to be induced to provide privileges, drugs, or favors for prisoners. Having a facility that is open to the public to come and visit also adds substantial extra expense in building the facility and in providing the added staff to manage it. And visitors also provide the likelihood that prisoners can direct illegal activities even while behind bars. The least expensive, and easiest to control, method of dealing with a population of violent people would be to confine each one separately. I know, it sounds like "throw them in the dungeon"! But it does not need to be inhumane. They can be provided with newspapers, magazines, books, and television. They can communicate with the outside world and with each other by telephone, mail, and internet, all of which can be monitored for dangerous content. Yes, people who commit acts of violence against their fellow man do give up their rights.

But, as for the "death penalty", I can not imagine that anyone has ever decided that committing a violent crime is worth while if they will spend the rest of their life in prison, but not if they may be executed. Not only does the death penalty not offer any additional deterrent effect, but the way it has been implemented in recent history tends to glorify the criminal, and marginalize the victim. Fifteen years after the crime, when the horrors of the crime have been long forgotten, the newspaper runs a picture of crowds of people protesting the execution of the woebegone criminal. There are interviews with his mother and his Boy Scout leader and his last words are printed under his picture. If anything, to a warped mind, this may give martyr or hero status to the criminal, and be a role model to emulate.

Also, there is the issue that people sometimes are wrongly convicted. And although years in prison for a crime that was not committed can never be restored, an improper imprisonment is still certainly more reversible that an improper execution! There also is, of course, a real moral issue with a society that puts people to death. How can we recoil in horror with societies that beat criminals bloody, or cut off their hands, or cut out their tongues, but yet we can approve of slaughtering them? All in all, with the high cost of appeal after appeal, many years of protracted court hearings, and the fact that it really does not accomplish anything more to deter crime than life imprisonment, society putting people to death doesn't make sense.

But what about the non-violent criminals: those who burglarize your house when you're away, steal your car, lift merchandise from the store, embezzle from their company, cheat on their taxes, plunder their companies leaving shareholders and pensioners destitute, abuse their position of public trust to enrich themselves with bribes and kick backs, or bilk little old ladies of their life savings. What to do about them? Although their crimes may be severe, there is a tendency to believe that we can take a chance on being able to reform them. Unlike the violent criminal, releasing them back into society when we believe that they will mend their ways does not seem to carry the same enormous risk of creating irreparable harm to future victims. Their ill-gotten gains should be confiscated and returned as restitution to their victims. Prison sentences should be sufficiently long and harsh to act as a deterrent to those who might contemplate a life of crime. For those with insufficient job skills to make an honest living, there needs to be in-prison vocational training programs to prepare them for life outside, with work release programs for a period of time prior to a total release. All need to be assisted with job placement upon release, and supervised with substantial monitoring for a considerable period of time after release to be sure that they remain gainfully employed and to help an adjustment into society. For those who have considerable skills, but simply chose to misuse them, a requirement for substantial community service might be appropriate, particularly if they can serve to counteract the harm they have done. For society to spend considerable amounts to try to reclaim these people is a very proper use of funds and certainly preferable to spending that money to keep them confined forever. But all must understand that this second chance for life is a precious gift. There will be no third chance. For those who, in spite of all efforts to help them reform, repeat their felonious way of life, there is no choice but to treat them as the violent criminals, and confine them for the rest of their lives.

CHAPTER 6
NARCOTIC DRUGS & OTHER
VICTIMLESS CRIMES

F or forty years now, we have been waging a "War on Drugs". We have spent unimaginable amounts of money, resources, and man power on this effort. We have imprisoned millions of people, with hundreds of thousands currently in prison. People guilty of no other crime than their addiction have had their lives devastated by being labeled a "felon", and spending years in prison. Those imprisonments have not in any way eliminated the problems of addiction to narcotic drugs. If anything, we have encouraged it. There is the allure of the "Forbidden Fruit". There is a tremendous financial incentive for drug pushers to create future customers, particularly among the young and the innocent. By keeping users outside the law, we make it vastly more difficult for them to seek treatment

And, of course, along with the problems of addiction, we have the problems of burglary, robbery, and muggings to get the money to afford the high cost of drugs. We have young women and young men engaged in prostitution to support their habits. We have addicts taking drugs of unknown quality and dosage and killing themselves.

We have created a nightmare for every parent: that their children will go off to school, and their classmates will introduce them to the world of "recreational" drugs. That their bright young ambitious children, with their lives in front of them, and a world of opportunity available to them, will be transformed into drug addicted zombies. In spite of, and quite possibly because of, our ridiculous policies regarding drugs, they are everywhere. The children will be exposed to both opportunity and peer pressure to experiment with drugs. And who knows what fine line is crossed from experimentation to a life of addiction and dependency. How many young lives have been destroyed by drug use?

We have created entire communities inside the United States, and entire foreign nations, where the primary industry is the production and distribution of narcotic drugs. In every major city in the United States, there are inner city neighborhoods which are controlled by those involved in the drug trade. There is rampant violence between rival dealers and rival gangs. Innocent bystanders are killed by stray bullets while walking down the street or sitting on their stoop. Little girls in Chicago recently have been killed by bullets crashing through their windows and through the walls of their own homes while they were quietly in bed and asleep. The situation bears an eerie resemblance to a period when the United States decided to deal with the problems of alcohol by making that substance illegal, thereby creating an era of powerful mobs and rampant violence.

The primary cash crops in Columbia are crops farmed to produce drugs to export primarily to the United States. The nation is run by the drug cartel, and the populace lives in dread. Mexico is plagued with drug trafficking, largely moving the drugs through to markets in the U.S. We have set Afghanistan free – free to produce record crops of the poppy plant. This finances the war lords who, with the money they derive from the drug trade, are more powerful than the Government, and threaten to undo whatever good we had accomplished there.

If we were to make narcotic drugs legally and readily available, it wouldn't eliminate drug addiction, but it would eliminate most of the other problems associated with this failed policy. We could have the drugs produced by major pharmaceutical companies, with known quality and dosage, under license from the government. The government would operate distribution outlets and make the drugs available to addicts at an affordable cost, or when necessary, at no cost. I can hear people protesting right now "but if we make drugs 'legal' we will be encouraging their use!" What Bullshit! These are the same people who protest that if we teach our children about sex, we will be encouraging fornication.

No, I'm not suggesting that packets of heroin be hanging next to the Juicy Fruit at the corner store. And I'm not advocating that K-Mart announce that opium is on the Blue-Light Special in Aisle 3. Nor should TV ads extol the pleasures of cocaine!

No, this is not a matter of allowing drugs to be merchandised, but of recognizing the reality that there are people who will find a way to get drugs and will find a way to fork over large amounts of money for those drugs, and there are those who will covet that money and will find a way to provide those drugs. The government needs to license the production of narcotic drugs and to create a not-for-profit distribution system to supply those who will otherwise be supplied by others. This needs to be done carefully, to make the drugs available to those intent in getting them, but not so easily available to encourage their use by the young and the curious. There would be Government operated facilities, located in areas where there are large concentrations of users, where small dosages would be supplied in a highly controlled manner.

And no, this is not a panacea. It will not eliminate all problems with narcotic drugs. There will still be drug users and drug addicts. Young people will still be tempted to experiment with drugs. But it will allow us to bring the problem inside the law and not outside the law, and to deal with it as a serious problem and not as a crime. We need to enter into serious educational programs to inform young people what drugs are all about before they reach the age of experimenting with them. No, "Just say No" is far from adequate. It has never worked as means of preventing sexual experimentation, it has never kept kids from experimenting with alcohol or tobacco, and it has never worked as a means of preventing experimentation with drugs, and it never will. Real knowledge, real understanding, and some real exposure to people who can relate real first hand experience may succeed far better. Removing the "illegal" label from drug use, may allow those young people who get caught up in drug experimentation to seek help and treatment.

And if we can eliminate the associated crime, the violence, the death through overdose and tainted drugs, and the imprisonment of hundreds of thousands of poor souls who are really not criminals, but are more to be pitied than blamed for their addictions, then we will have accomplished a lot.

From where we are today, this transformation will not be easy. The plan is to put the existing drug farmers, the drug factories, and the drug dealers out of business. These people will not give up their way of life easily. To the extent possible, it may make the transition easier if some of the same people currently involved in the illegal farming, and distribution of drugs illegally can be employed in doing these same activities in a controlled legal manner.

I don't mean to minimize the problems that would be associated with this radical switch of policy. Buying and pedaling drugs is a way of life, and the economic lifeblood of many communities. It will be extraordinarily difficult to reorganize these populations around legitimate and productive pursuits. This is true both within the United States and in a number of foreign countries where growing and processing narcotic drugs and smuggling them to the United States is a primary industry. There will be substantial violence, and violence against the system intended to supplant them. It will take armed guards to protect the facilities producing the drugs, and the facilities distributing the drugs. It will take years, or decades, to undo the damage we have done with this failed policy of trying to eliminate drug use through trying to eliminate the supply.

There are other victimless crimes which we have similarly attempted to deal with by criminalizing activities between willing adult participants. Prostitution is among them. Treating prostitution as a crime is a way of clogging up courts and prisons while not dealing with the very real problems. Young women are coerced into the life, and are controlled and abused by their madams and by their procurers. Prostitution is a source for spreading crippling and deadly disease. Would it not be far better to legalize and regulate, to require registration and frequent medical exams, to attempt to protect both the prostitutes and the customers from abuse and disease? As with the narcotic drugs, criminalizing the behavior does not eliminate it, nor necessarily even reduce it, but it does place participants outside the law, and makes it impossible to address all of the problems attendant to it. Decriminalizing prostitution does not mean that any of us approve of it, but it may give us the ability to regulate, to control, and to find means of reducing the side effects.

Gambling is still classified as a crime in most places. It seems particularly absurd, in that once the states came to realize that they could make a great deal of money off of it, they became the primary "numbers" racketeers. And any law to prevent others from running numbers seems just like an abuse of power in an attempt to eliminate competition. Similarly, if the state can authorize Off Track Betting Parlors or allow gambling on river boats where they can take a rake off the pool, what is their justification for prohibiting other bookies from taking bets, or allowing people to shoot craps in the alley? Now that the states are the biggest promoters of legalized gambling, it seems like the height of hypocrisy that there should be laws criminalizing gambling. Not that gambling isn't a problem. But regulating gambling to be sure that it is honest is easier done if it falls within the law, and not outside of it. But even honest institutionalized gambling is a sucker's game – players know going in that the game is rigged against them. And yet, somehow, it seems to hold great appeal for a great many people. And for a significant portion of those, its appeal becomes thoroughly addictive, and ruinous. What is needed is not criminalization, which has never prevented gambling anyway, but reasonable programs to attempt to set limits to prevent compulsive gambling behavior. What is needed is public education and treatment to deal with those for whom gambling has become an uncontrollable obsession.

CHAPTER 7
GUNS

Twenty thousand people in the US are murdered each year by guns. Hundreds of thousands of people are shot, robbed, raped, mugged, or otherwise traumatized by people with guns. Entire communities live in fear of stray bullets hitting bystanders or crashing through walls and windows. Fortunately the guns and ammunition generally used for mayhem are not the guns and ammunition used for sport.

There are many millions of Americans for whom hunting, skeet shooting, and other target shooting are a major form of recreation. It would be wrong to impinge on their freedom to enjoy their sport as a means of attempting to keep guns out of the hands of those who misuse them. None of us want to live in a society where we are so scared that we have to give up our freedom to pursue our lives in order to attempt to eliminate all risks to our safety – that would be a bad trade.

But there are many guns, and many forms of ammunition, that are not designed for sport, but are designed specifically for killing humans. We do not need Uzis for sport. We do not need assault weapons with enormous magazines capable of firing a hundred rounds in a minute for sport. We do not need hollow point bullets, armor piercing bullets, or explosive ammunition for sport. We do not need "Saturday Night Specials" for sport.

Yes, I know that "it isn't guns that kill". It is people with guns that kill. And yes, I can certainly relate to those who say "I take care of my guns, why do you want to interfere with my rights?" And the answer is: I don't want to interfere with your rights. But the only way we can remove guns from those who use them to terrorize, maim, and kill the rest of us, is to remove them from everyone. As with most things, what we end up with is a compromise. Remove the guns that are the most likely to be lethal to humans, and don't interfere with the rights of those who want to have their guns for sport.

We should ban private ownership of all guns and all ammunition except for those rifles and shotguns and ammunition commonly used for sport and hunting. We should ban their manufacture, import or sale. We should make it illegal to possess any guns except sporting guns, and offer to buy all privately owned existing guns and ammunition of the varieties banned, at fair market price. Buy up all the inventories in all the stores that sell guns and ammunition. Convert all the factories in the U.S. currently manufacturing the banned guns and ammunition to other purposes, and compensate owners and employees for what ever loss they may incur from this. Restrictions, waiting periods, background checks, and all the other maze of regulations currently in effect creates a lot of red tape and a lot of nuisance to legitimate gun users and does nothing to eliminate guns from the hands of those who use them to intimidate, to commit crimes, or to kill their fellow man.

And by all means, make any crime committed using a gun to threaten another person, whether or not the gun is actually fired, an offense to be punishable by imprisonment for the rest of the criminal's life. If a criminal says "your money or your life", we must take him at his word, and assume that he would actually shoot someone in order to steal a few dollars. He can not be allowed to continue to be free in society.

But what about the second amendment: "A well regulated Militia, being necessary to the security of a free State, the right of the people to keep and bear arms, shall not be infringed." No one can be sure what the writers of that amendment had in mind, but it was lifted from the Virginia Bill of Rights published on June 12, 1776, and largely authored by Thomas Jefferson. In it, the meaning may be a little clearer: "That a well regulated militia, composed of the body of the people, trained to arms, is the proper, natural, and safe defense of a free state; that standing armies, in time of peace, should be avoided, as dangerous to liberty; and that, in all cases, the military should be under strict subordination to, and governed by, the civil power". The intention was that, in order to avoid having standing armies, the populace would have guns so that they could be called to duty when a militia was required for the defense of the state or to quell a civil unrest.

It is highly unlikely that the Founding Fathers thought it a good idea that everyone should be packing heat so that in a fit of road rage they could go teach that m…f …er that cut them off and flipped them the bird, a lesson they would never forget. Nor did they think we needed Uzis to spray bullets at the house of a rival gang member. Or to protect our turf from the rival drug dealer from the other side of town. Or that some freak kid could take his dad's guns to school, and blow his classmates away.

It seems that daily, the paper has tragic stories of innocent kids killed or maimed by stray bullets. Stories of kids who shot themselves or a playmate with the gun dad had next to the headboard "for protection". Shopkeepers in "bad parts of town" must risk their lives daily just to earn an honest living, and all of them have from time to time come face to face with an armed person who would kill them for the few dollars in the till, or just because they can.

But what about the need for a gun for protection? There are daily stories about the horrors inflicted by guns, on purpose, by accident, or in a fit of pique, or people putting a bullet through their own head in a moment of depression, but when was the last time you read a story about someone actually successfully defending themselves from an attacker because they had a gun for protection? And are you really less likely to get harmed by an attacker if you are somehow able to go for your gun and attempt to confront the attacker with it? Actually, there are articles on the subject that claim you are several times more likely to be injured or killed because you have a gun in the house than you are to successfully defend yourself with it. But it is a subject that needs real impartial study, and reliable statistics. Is this not something that, as a matter of public good, should be commissioned by government?

Now I'm not suggesting that a ban and recall of all non-sporting guns and ammunition will really make them all disappear. There are more than one hundred million guns and hundreds of millions of rounds of ammunition, that I am suggesting banning, currently in the hands of the public. They will not all be turned in. And there will still be black market manufacture and importation, but on a vastly smaller scale than what is currently available. Those with money and connections will still be able to buy any kind of gun, and be able to buy hollow point, armor piercing, or whatever other ammunition they want, but it will become scarcer and scarcer. Those who have guns and ammunition will horde them. A determined individual will still be able to get them, but they won't be in the hands of every kid who wants to shoot his classmates, and they won't be in the hands of every street punk who wants to have a gun tucked in the waist band of his jeans to show his macho manhood. Every hot head who might use a gun in a moment of anger won't have one. And thousands of kids won't be shot or grow up orphans.

CHAPTER 8
TORT LAW

We have developed a society that loves to sue. And we are encouraged in this by lawyers who love to sue. And the reason, of course, is that there is BIG MONEY in suing. If a person is injured by the wanton, willful, careless, or negligent acts of another, certainly they are entitled to be compensated for their injury. And that is true whether the injury is to their property, their reputation, or physical injury to their body. But we have lost sight of the concept of compensation for the loss, and have been convinced that the true purpose of suing is to punish. And that is where the big money, and the big fees for lawyers, comes in.

In business suits, it is well established that the amount of compensation you may seek is the amount you have lost due to the actions of the liable party. You have to actually enumerate and prove the amount of the damage.

But in personal tort suits, it is another story. If someone is found to be liable for a physical injury sustained by another person, and that injury prevents them from being able to work at their career for the rest of their life, it is a terrible tragedy. The liable party should be required to provide for the cost of all the medical treatment that will be required, and to provide for replacing all of the lost income. These may be some very large amounts of money. If the injured person could reasonably have been expected to earn $50,000 a year with annual increases of 5% for the next thirty years, and is expected to require medical treatments amounting to another $50,000 a year, the liable person should be required to provide an annuity that will provide those amounts. And the attorneys are entitled to receive reasonable fees for their work in determining the liability of the parties, and the amounts that should be required to compensate the injured person for his financial loss.

But then we introduce another concept – "Pain & Suffering". There is no way to put a dollar figure on pain and suffering. How many dollars would someone have to offer you to make you feel that it would be worth it to cut off the little finger of your left hand? There is no amount high enough to adequately compensate you even for that injury. And for more severe injuries? The sky is the limit. Or if the liable party has "deep pockets", even the sky is not a high enough limit. For relatively minor injuries, we have suits for tens of millions of dollars. If McDonalds made the coffee too hot, we have to teach them a lesson, and give the poor victim forty or fifty million dollars. And, of course, the attorneys get fifteen or twenty million too. And that creates an enormous incentive to look for situations where a suit with potentially gigantic awards can be filed and pursued.

And the unlimited awards apply not only for physical damage. How much is your reputation worth? And if your reputation is damaged, will you really suffer monetary damages? And can you really compute the amount of those damages? But particularly with celebrities, it is easy to claim extraordinary amounts of damage for any minor affront. A story they don't like. An unauthorized and unflattering photo. For entertainers, it has been said that there is no such thing as bad publicity. And to be sure, the law suit creates more publicity over the alleged affront and helps to further hype the impression that anyone can sue anyone for any amount.

And if a lawyer can't find a quadriplegic to represent, or a tarnished celebrity reputation, they may be able to find some company with deep pockets and find some way in which they can allege that the company has damaged millions of customers. With a potential litigation for tens of millions of dollars, perhaps the company will settle for a few million. The lawyer can pocket a couple million, and have checks for 37¢ sent out to a million "class action clients".

And we all pay the tab. We pay for it when the cost of liability insurance is added in to the price of the products we buy. We pay for it in the cost of our automobile insurance and homeowners insurance. And we pay for it big time in the cost of our health care. It's not as though the enormous awards paid out for malpractice suits actually weeds out the bad doctors, or improves our health care. Any doctor, or any facility, in the health care industry carries insurance to cover these costs. And the cost of the insurance is just added to our bills.

It is high time we revert to a system of computing monetary awards based on real monetary damage. It is high time we pass some legislation defining the rules for class action suits. It is high time we stop treating the filing of law suits as though they were the equivalent of playing the lottery.

And if not by awarding gigantic amounts of money to an individual (and his attorneys) for a lawsuit, how do we deter companies from engaging in reckless, harmful, or destructive practices? How do we weed out doctors who practice bad medicine? Those should be matters for public policy. Companies illegally, deliberately, or negligently endangering the public should be subject to criminal action. They should be subject to fines sufficient to prevent such behavior. The money from those fines would go into the public coffers for the benefit of the public, not into the pockets of individuals, and indirectly paid by the public. And if fines are not sufficient to prevent dangerous practices, in extreme cases, criminal action can be brought against individuals within the companies for actions disregarding the public welfare. Doctors suspected of practicing bad medicine should be subject to review by a board of professionals competent to make informed judgment, to determine if disciplinary action, including rescinding their license to practice, should be invoked.

CHAPTER 9
TRAFFIC

We are all painfully familiar with the traffic policeman sitting in his car on a side street with his radar gun waiting for someone to drive thirty five miles per hour in a twenty five mile per hour zone, or failing to rock back after stopping at the stop sign. That practice does not, in fact, really deal with dangerous driving habits, and tends to promote disrespect among the public for police in general.

We are also painfully familiar with driving down a crowded expressway doing the sixty five mile per hour limit while people are weaving to and fro across three lanes of traffic, squeezing between cars where there are gaps scarcely big enough to fit through, trying to do eighty. Driver's safety instructors call for leaving a two second gap between cars under ideal conditions. At sixty five miles per hour that is a gap of 190 feet, or about 12 car lengths. But instead, there are drivers tailgating within a whisker of the car ahead. If that car ahead of them suddenly brakes for a piece of debris in the road, they will be through their windshield and the back window of the car ahead before they can begin to move a foot to a brake. The other day I passed a pile-up on the expressway of seven cars. When the first car stopped suddenly, six more piled into it in broad daylight on dry pavement. Every winter you can read about pile-ups on I-70 through the Colorado Rockies where twenty or thirty vehicles have plowed into each other! Other drivers are driving erratically and showing signs of inebriation. Others are driving at forty miles per hour in the left lane, forcing traffic to pass to the right, causing an equally hazardous situation. And then there are young men on motorcycles literally racing each other on a crowded highway and weaving between the moving traffic. And the highways are littered with the carnage daily.

What is really needed is a much greater presence of police driving the highways in plain clothes in innocuous unmarked cars. The cars could be equipped with cameras front and rear to record the behaviors observed. We also could make use of cameras placed on bridges, towers, or other observation points to identify and record the actions of the really dangerous drivers. Technology certainly exists to be able to blow up pictures of license plates and even drivers' faces to identify who they are. The emphasis needs to shift away from a game of "Gotcha", writing tickets and collecting local revenue. We need to replace that with a real effort to identify the dangerous drivers and either re-train them and correct their actions, or remove them from the streets.

Perhaps we could make some significant reduction of the forty thousand people who are killed, and hundreds of thousands who are injured, on our highways each year.

Another subject that needs attention is the extreme danger posed by young people just starting their careers as drivers. We are all aware that young drivers have accidents, and severe accidents, at a rate several times that of older drivers. Just how much of the problem is their lack of experience, and how much is their youthful exuberance and lack of mature judgment, is an open question. I know that in the first couple of years after I started to drive, I cracked up more cars than I have in all the years since. I was a disaster. I can still remember my first accident, and the feeling a moment before, knowing that I was about to crash. I was driving along a side street through a residential area, and I blew through a stop sign. At the time I was sure that the fault lay with a tree that had grown to obscure the sign – damned tree, it should know better. More experienced drivers, of course, know that when driving down a street such as that, that cross traffic can not be seen until you are at the intersection, and it is necessary to pause and check for oncoming cars and pedestrians at each intersection regardless of stop signs, yield signs, or no signs. There were others caused simply by having insufficient familiarity with the vehicle. Like the night I was driving with a car full of friends. When a light turned red, I hit the brakes too hard on the rain slicked pavement, and did a 360 in the intersection – miraculously hitting nothing. Or the time I pulled up in front of a girl friend's house, and clipped her dad's car. That would have been the most mortifying of my young driving experiences, were it not for the time at college when I was pulling into the driveway of a sorority house and turned to wave to a girl I knew – yes, I plowed into the decorative stone gate post at the entrance to the drive!

There are a number of steps that can be taken to radically improve the performance of young drivers. Requiring that young drivers must take a course of driving instruction with professional instructors including a substantial amount of on-the-road driving experience is a good step. A permit that only allows the new driver to drive while accompanied by a responsible adult for the first six months of driving is also a big help. Restricting young drivers from driving at night, and restricting the number of other young people that can be in their car for the first couple years after they begin driving has been found to make a huge difference in serious accident rates. And it might make kids stop and think if they know that if they are found driving with any level of intoxication, their driving career will be postponed for another two years. The kids will scream and yell, protest how unfair it all is, and hate us – but a great many more of them will live to become adults.

On a less serious, but still important subject having to do with traffic management: three quarters of all traffic signal lights do not need to be operating more than a few hours a day, and not at all on weekends. We all sit far too often for what seems like an eternity, watching an empty intersection, and waiting for a light to turn green. Surely the technology exists to equip signal lights with clocks, and to set them flashing red one direction and yellow the other during the hours and days when they are not needed. Does no one involved in traffic management engineering care? Is our wasted time of no value? Do we race to beat the red light to avoid the wait, and endanger ourselves and others? And does the irritation manifest itself in hazardous driving? What about the millions of gallons of fuel unnecessarily burned, and the tons of pollutants unnecessarily dumped into the atmosphere? Is it time to make this into an issue?

And on a similar subject, while driving during rush hour traffic today along Irving Park Road, a main arterial road in a Chicago suburb, traffic was halted while a mile long northbound train crept at <u>ten</u> miles an hour across the road. When it eventually cleared the grade crossing, the gate rose and six cars passed through, before the gates lowered again for the southbound train. This one was going <u>five</u> miles an hour. Is it really necessary to let the railroads have complete free rein with regards to their ability to block traffic?

CHAPTER 10
FREE SPEECH

There are many widely recognized and accepted limitations on "free speech". There is the classic "you can not yell "Fire!" in the crowded theater". You also can not tell lies to injure a person's reputation. You also can not stand in front of the angry crowd and holler "let's go get the son-of-a bitch and hang him from that tree". You can not say to your friend "let's go plant a bomb in the Synagogue". Nor can you tell the black man that he can not eat in your restaurant. And you can not tell the pretty young girl in the office that you can get her a promotion if she will sleep with you - you can't even look at her and comment "nice tits". Yes, libel, slander, inciting a riot, conspiring to commit a felony, depriving a person of their civil rights, and sexual harassment are all well accepted limitations on "free speech".

So just where do we draw the lines? Is it really necessary to allow a group to march or demonstrate preaching hatred and bigotry? When does allowing them to spew their bile result in causing others to commit acts of violence? When does subjecting a group to insults, or instilling the fear of acts of violence against them, constitute a breach of their civil right to live with dignity and in peace? Would donning white robes and pointy hoods and burning crosses on lawns be just an expression of a political opinion, and be protected by a guarantee of "free speech"? Is marching with swastikas and signs praising Hitler the expression of a political opinion?

No, it isn't easy. Sometimes the lines are quite blurred. But that is why we have courts and judges. And the assumption that you can derogate any group in any manner under a guise that you are simply exercising a right of "free speech" needs to be examined. Other countries that are generally noted for their attitude embracing a free society nevertheless have laws restricting hateful speech. Recently, a Swiss court convicted Dogu Perincek, leader of the Turkish Workers Party in Switzerland, for violating the Anti-Racism law when he proclaimed that the mass murder of Armenians during the World War was not genocide. It is not easy to clearly write into law the specifics of what can and can not be said or done, but like many other laws, it revolves around intent. If a group gathers to demonstrate with the intent of causing people of a particular race, religion, or nationality to feel that they should be afraid for their safety or their lives, then that should be illegal. If a group gathers and demonstrates with the intent of promulgating amongst the population at large, an irrational hatred of people of a particular race, religion, or nationality, that should be illegal. If a group gathers and demonstrates with the foreseeable result that members will commit future acts of violence, that should be illegal. One of the problems that has been pointed out about enforcement of statutes to bar a group from assembling is that it might require prejudging what a group intends to do before they have actually done it. However, once a group has engaged in actions prohibited by these laws, it should certainly be possible for the court to examine what they have done, and issue an order prohibiting them from repeating the offensive behavior, with criminal penalties if they disregard the ruling.

There are other areas under the general heading of "Free Speech" which, while not of the same magnitude of problem as those discussed so far, nevertheless bear examination. Although a person may have a right to speak, that does not convey an obligation for the rest of us to have to listen. It has been argued that advertising and the solicitation of contributions for someone's favorite charity or favorite politician are expressions of free speech. And that their right to free speech therefore gives them the right to use your telephone to annoy you anytime night or day, to run pop-up ads that pop-up while you are trying to use your computer, or to fill your e-mail with spam and drivel. Although these may be minor annoyances, they are repeated millions of times daily. If you have the misfortune of getting on widely circulated lists, your phone may ring with solicitations 8 or 10 or more times daily. Pop-up ads can make the act of trying to research a topic on the internet a miserable experience. Although we have installed filters to dump most of it into "junk" folders, my e-mail at work receives about 100 spam solicitations a day. Is there any reasonable justification why legislation prohibiting these forms of unauthorized and unwanted use of your telephone, and of your computer, should not be enacted, with fines for non-compliance sufficient to make these activities uneconomic?

And does "free speech" really require that anyone may make any claim for any product without any testing or proof of the claims? If I take their pills, will I really get thinner without diet or exercise? Will I really grow hair? Will my penis really grow larger? Do they really have evidence of an ability to predict that a stock price is about to triple? Aren't some of these claims quite dangerous to those follow their untested and unproven health advice, and forego mainstream treatment from Doctors, Dieticians, or other knowledgeable professionals? How many people have lost their savings following the "Get Rich Quick" schemes? And aren't all of these bogus claims a fraud, bilking money from victims by promising something they won't deliver, the same as any other fraud? Why shouldn't there be legislation making it illegal to make claims for a product without testing and evidence to support the claims, and with fines and possible imprisonment for those who prey upon a naive public?

CHAPTER 11
HEALTH CARE

W e have the best health care in the world that no one can afford.

I don't really know just why health care costs have been inflating by 10% per year when the economy has been inflating less than 3%. In 1960, the cost of health care was less than 5% of our Nation's Gross Domestic Product. Today it is more than 15% of GDP. In proportion to all our other costs of living, it has tripled, and is continuing to soar! It was not that long ago that every company large and small could readily provide every employee with full health insurance coverage, and for a few dollars per pay check they could sign on to cover their families. But over the past forty years, that has become an impossibility. Yes, we have equipment, procedures, and treatments that were unimaginable 40 years ago, but how many of us are better off, and how many are in fact worse off, because they do not have access even to basic health care?

And therefore, there are many of us who do not have checkups, do not practice preventative health care, and do not seek treatment for ailments when they might be easily treated. People who wait until they require emergency treatment, and then show up at hospital emergency rooms. This is a triple whammy. The hospital emergency room would be the most expensive place for treatment under any circumstances. The fact that they have waited until their condition has deteriorated has substantially increased the cost of treatment. And they may die, or be left with long term ill effects that might have been avoidable. The high cost of this emergency room treatment, of course, ends up being shared by all of us in the cost of hospital services, and in our health insurance premiums.

And among those without insurance and being treated in hospital emergency rooms are the twelve million undocumented aliens living here. But that's a topic for another chapter.

What else is driving the cost of health care to skyrocket? How much of it is linked to our propensity to sue the doctor and sue the facility and sue anyone else we can think of if we don't like the result of our medical treatment. And those who sue receive humongous awards, and the premiums for mal-practice insurance soar, and those costs are, of course, passed on to you and to me. And beyond the actual cost of the mal-practice insurance premiums is that the potential for litigation hanging over every medical treatment causes the doctors and the facilities to practice defensive medicine. More tests, more opinions, more consultations than would otherwise be reasonable, but is necessary to protect themselves if the patient sues.

And how much of it is due to the fact that health care is just not very responsive to the market pressures and competition that keep the price of other goods and services in line? If you need to get you car repaired, you get a quotation of the cost before proceeding. You can negotiate it, or shop it somewhere else. But if your body needs to be repaired, that is just not practical. And if medications are patented, there is no competition. And what is the limit to how much a drug can cost if you are told that if you don't have it you will die?

And then there is the advent of categorizing every quirk as a "condition" requiring treatment. My wife is a school teacher, and to hear her tell it, there is scarcely a kid in the entire school that isn't classified with some kind of a "condition" - Learning Disability, ADD, ADHD, BD, etc., etc., and many are prescribed Ritalin, anti-depressants such as Prozac, and the anti-psychotic drug Risperdal. When we were kids, we were all just "kids". You saw a Doctor when you got sick, not to diagnose your "condition". If Tom Sawyer, that rascally literary hero, were alive and in a US school today, he would likely be given a pill to rein in his mischievous habits, from squirming out of chores to skipping class. (Agence France-Presse 9/8/01)

But I expect that the largest contributor to the rapidly escalating costs of medical care has to do with our treatment of the aged. Every old person has a bunch of doctors. Specialists for this and that and the other, each prescribing a bunch of pills, and some prescribing pills to counteract the other pills. Old people start off their day by opening the appropriate cover in their seven day pill box, or if one box isn't large enough, perhaps two or three seven day pill boxes. And then they can spend the rest of the day going from doctor to doctor. But it gets much worse in the last few months of life. We have learned to do extraordinary things to extend life for a few more months, at enormous cost. I have been through this with several family members. Moving the dying person in and out of hospitals, performing exhaustive tests and numerous procedures, moving to nursing homes between hospital stays, and eventually to hospice care. It is possible to spend hundreds of thousands of dollars in this procedure, and some time well before it is over, the patient recognizes that they have no quality of life, and no hope for recovery, and even they become anxious to have it over. Several times, my Dad asked along the way, "let me go". This is not an easy decision when it is someone you love, but the fact is, we all will die. And in some way or another, those hundreds of thousands of dollars are going to drive up the cost of health care for all of us to the point that young healthy people who could really benefit from a doctor's care will be unable to afford to get the treatment they need and deserve.

So what is the answer? The answer is universal cradle to grave basic health care for all Americans, funded by our taxes. We have such a complex and mystifying patchwork of health care programs now that no one can comprehend them. All we know is that the cost is prohibitive and becoming more so day by day. We need to establish a sound and sane medical care plan to cover the basic medical needs of all Americans, to be administered by the companies currently in the health insurance business, and this plan should definitely be tailored around cost. The basic plan should be drafted by a panel consisting of doctors, medical facility administrators, and health insurance experts. It most likely will result in setting up numerous twenty-four hour health care clinics, and providing much of the care with nurses and medics, with doctors available as needed. Based on a cost-benefit analysis by the panel, the basic plan may exclude numerous tests and procedures that have become common over the past few decades, but that have driven medical costs to the level where they are today. The plan would cover prescribed medications, but again, with severe guidelines as to what medications are really necessary and cost justified. The toughest area to write into the basic policy will be "end of life" treatment procedures. Hideously tough decisions, but necessary.

For those who want and can afford more options, the companies would sell supplemental policies, much as they do for Medicare today. Or for those who want no part of this system, they may opt out, provide privately for their own health care, and receive a tax credit equal to the cost-per-person for the program. But the cost of whatever extra medical options that they wish to have available to them will have to be fully incorporated in the cost of their program, and must not spill over in to the costs for the rest of us.

So how do we afford this? We already are paying for it. Somebody is! And who else would it be? All that I am talking about is to simplify the plan, reduce the complexities, and have a comprehensive program aimed at providing the most necessary medical care at a cost we can afford. It may be all well and good to talk about how "no amount of money is too much when my life is at stake", but reality is, that we have already arrived at a point where many lives are being sacrificed because we have made the cost of health care unaffordable. And if we continue on the path we are on, it will just keep getting worse and worse.

CHAPTER 12
PUBLIC EDUCATION

Do we really want to direct public education to the least capable students who are most likely to be "left behind"? In fact, we are leaving many of their little behinds undereducated, unfulfilled, and unprepared for the world they live in. The number of kids who can not effectively read, write, or perform basic arithmetic is appalling. The drop out rates from the Nation's high schools a tragedy. The fact is that there are many kids who are not suited for general education. And for those who are not, we need more emphasis on career / job based training – where they will see the relevance and be more likely to stay with the program.

This does not mean that they are not talented. My Labrador Retriever Jake can calculate the trajectory of a Frisbee and time his leap to snatch it in mid-air in his teeth – a feat few humans would even attempt! If we are walking in the woods and the bet is between Jake or my wife to know the path back to the trail head, it's no contest. He is a wonderfully talented dog. But he is a dog! I don't expect to discuss Nietzsche with him.

A number of years ago the Chicago Bears drafted a stand-out Option Quarterback from Kansas named Bobby Douglass. He was an amazingly talented athlete. When he rolled out, he was a true triple threat. He could pitch the ball out, throw it downfield, or pulverize the defense with his running speed and power. But the Bears wanted him to stand in the pocket. Well, he wasn't Johnny Unitas, he was Bobby Douglass! And instead of developing the talents he had, the Bears gave up on him, and, wasted his fabulous potential.

The one-size-fits-all model for education does not fit all. For those who are not going on to a college and planning to become doctors, lawyers, accountants, business executives, scientists, teachers, philosophers or otherwise engage in a career requiring broad based and extensive education, it may be far more effective to combine actual work experience and education in an apprentice program, and develop the talents and abilities that the individual does have. Depending on their career choice, they may come to see the need for some of the education they otherwise found boring and were willing to forsake. If they want a career in the construction trades, as a toolmaker, or as a mechanic, they will find that the ability to read and write are vital, and that a fair amount of mathematics, geometry, and ability to read blueprints and schematics, convert decimals and fractions and conversion to metrics, are all vital skills. If they are considering a career in retail, it will be necessary to do data input, read inventory spread sheets, and, of course, to deal with money and some basic accounting. There is nothing like spending time in the real world, in a dead end job, to wake kids up and give them an appreciation for doing what it takes to provide themselves the knowledge, skills, and gumption required to live a more fulfilling life.

And for those who do have the intelligence, intellectual curiosity, thirst for knowledge, and burning desire to excel and achieve, we should devote far more of our educational efforts to them. We should not be "dumbing down" the curriculum to cater to students who can not or will not benefit from it. We need to offer to our best and our brightest the greatest educational opportunities possible. This should be true through all grades, and we need to be certain that advanced education is available for all who are eager and qualified, and that none are excluded from a lack of funding. If we are going to maintain our status as a great society, it is these kids who will propel us and lead us in the future.

Also, for all students, we need to increase education for the skills required to live in society – how to get a job, open a bank account, borrow money, deal with credit cards, understand interest and compound interest, pay bills, buy and use insurance. What do you do in a job interview, how do you dress, how do you prepare, and how do you conduct yourself? How do you rent an apartment? Read the lease? Place a security deposit, and protect yourself so that it will be returned when the lease term is complete? How do you buy a house? Read the contracts, arrange a mortgage? What is a credit report? And how do you check on yours, preserve good credit, and why is that vital? How do you file a tax return and pay taxes? How do you invest? What are mutual funds, ETFs, how do bonds work, money market funds, and compound interest? How and when do you start preparing for the money you will want in retirement? When should you consult with an attorney, a CPA, an investment adviser, or other professionals, and how do you choose them?

And we certainly need to increase education on basic hygiene, how often to have a medical check up, dental check up, eye exam, and how to make sure that all required inoculations are up to date. We need to learn about nutrition and exercise to keep our bodies fit and healthy. We need to be taught about addictive drugs, alcohol, tobacco, gambling, and other addictive substances and behaviors, with in depth study of the nightmares that lie ahead for those who succumb to these addictions.

And dealing with kids who are approaching puberty, isn't it imperative that we have discussions regarding sexuality. Teach the dangers of sexual experimentation, both from a physical and an emotional point of view. And teach the devastating affects of sexually transmitted diseases. And the devastation to a young person's life that comes from having a pregnancy at far too early an age. Knowing full well that despite any ministrations against it, some kids will be sexually active; they need to be taught methods to prevent the spread of disease. And they need to be taught the methods available to prevent conception.

Do we simply assume that somehow kids will know about life? How many will get themselves into serious trouble with debt, with buying things they can not afford, with people taking advantage of their youth and naïveté and susceptibility to swindles, with lack of protecting their health, with addictions, and with unplanned and unwanted pregnancies?

CHAPTER 13
TAXES & EMPLOYMENT TAXES

From an employer's perspective, there is a cost to having an employee, and it doesn't matter whether the cost is in the wage rate, or in the other costs of employment. Even for people making minimum wage, 7.65% is deducted from their wages for FICA, and the employer pays another 7.65% for FICA. The employer generally pays about 5% in unemployment insurance, and 7% or 8% in workmen's compensation insurance, some 28% costs added to the take-home pay of the lowest paid workers. This is an incredibly regressive tax system. Although eliminating those taxes on low paid workers would not make their cost as low as the cost of some workers abroad, it certainly could be a substantial factor in favor of keeping some jobs in the U.S. Why should the workers with the lowest incomes be paying the costs for these programs intended for the general benefit of society, rather than people with the greatest incomes? Why should people making their money as a return-on-investment rather than by working for it, not pay these costs at all?

If we remove the burden of those employment taxes from the employers of production workers, we might find that it creates an enormous economic boon to all of us, finding that we can actually return a substantial number of manufacturing jobs to the United States. And certainly we have to question: can the United States really maintain its dominant position in the world, as a nation that doesn't manufacture? Was the British Empire based on their early lead in the Industrial Revolution, and their dominance as producers of manufactured goods? Did the United States rise to its position of dominance as a result of our manufacturing prowess? Did our position as the dominant inventors, innovators, and discoverers of most of the technologies that define modern life – pioneering efforts in electricity, telephones, recording sound, photography and moving pictures, automobiles, airplanes, television, and computers – all arise from our dominant position as manufacturers? Did our preeminence in educating scientists and engineers arise from the needs and opportunities of American industry? Will the decline and fall of American power be precipitated by our transformation to a nation that is dependent on the rest of the world to supply us all of our most basic needs? Can a "Super Power" be a nation of burger flippers and personal trainers?

Social Security was originally pitched as though it were a savings program for retirement – that the money the employee puts in will grow, and be returned when he retires. It isn't so. In fact, the money he puts in immediately goes out to his retired father. Or someone else's retired father. Social Security and Medicare really exist as social programs – we as a society recognize that we have a responsibility to support our elders, and not have them begging in the street. As such, there is really no rationale as to why the qualification for benefits, and the amount of benefits, should be tied to an individual's work history. Other pension plans or savings and investments accrue and grow as a person works and earns and saves, to provide for their retirement. Social Security is a floor, a minimum amount to support those who have no other means of support. The funding for Social Security should be part of the general tax revenue, and be paid for by the wealthiest, not by the poorest, members of society.

"Free Enterprise", or "Capitalism", has a lot to recommend it as an economic system. It offers each individual the freedom to choose whatever career path suits their interest, ambition and abilities, free to pursue their passions, free to go wherever and do whatever is to their liking, restrained only by economic realities. It offers enormous incentive for invention, innovation, and hard work, with the fruits of one's labors accruing to the person who has created them. Our economic system has created a highly productive and fabulously wealthy economy. Competition tends to assure that products will be produced in the varieties and styles and quality levels desired by the consuming public, and that prices will be in line with costs.

However, the down side is that a vastly disproportionate amount of the wealth can accrue to a relatively few individuals, and not necessarily to those who are responsible for creating the products and methods that have produced this wealth. Entertainers, for example, including actors, musicians, professional athletes, and some who achieve celebrity status without any particular talent other than a talent for celebrity, are able to achieve incredible amounts of wealth. Some lawyers, who have found a niche where they are dealing with who will control vast sums of money, are able to create vast sums of money for themselves. Chief executives tend to achieve "star" status, and are hired by companies with billions in revenues, companies that they did not create nor build. And these executives are paid enormous amounts in salaries, bonuses, stock options, and then they receive more money in "golden parachutes" that are paid to them when it turns out that they have made a mess of running the company and are dismissed.

It would be a mistake to create a tax system that would remove the ability of the free market to operate, that would remove the incentive for people to strive to make money. But it is those who have expendable incomes beyond their needs who have the ability to fund the government, and to fund the social programs that make us a compassionate society. And if the very wealthy pay a greater share of the burden, they will still have plenty of incentive for their efforts, they will still have far more than they need, and no, they will not have been treated unfairly. And we might find that we all create greater wealth as a society, and preserve greater independence as a nation, by shifting more of the burden to those with the ability to bear it.

On another, but related subject, the method of collecting taxes by having an incredibly complex set of rules for calculating incomes and deductions, and having more than one hundred thirty million people filing Individual Income Tax Returns, is an incredible waste of time and effort. There is an entire industry built around tax preparation, and every American spends hours preparing and filing tax returns. Every company has to calculate, collect, and remit withholding tax for every employee from every pay check. And there is an army of IRS agents required to process and review those hundred thirty million returns. It also pits Americans against their own government – the "Tax Collector" is a favorite villain in cartoons and comedy. A far easier and more efficient method of taxation would be to exempt the vast majority of people from filing income taxes, and instead institute a national sales tax. Nearly all retailers are already set up to calculate, collect and remit sales taxes for their state, and sometimes local, governments. It would be virtually no additional burden upon them to also collect a national sales tax, and it is easy to monitor and administer. In order to shift more of the burden on to those who can afford it, different items could be taxed at different rates. For instance, basic necessities such as groceries might be taxed at only 3%, luxury goods being taxed at higher rates. Even different classes of the same category could be taxed at different rates. Fast food restaurants and sandwich shops where the average meal costs less than $5, might be taxed at 5%, family restaurants where the average meal costs $5 to $15 might be taxed at 8%, with rates climbing as the relative luxury of the restaurant increases, to perhaps 25% for restaurants serving $35 ala carte entrees and $300 bottles of wine. Similarly, automobiles providing basic transportation, and selling for less than $10,000 might be taxed at 5%, with rates climbing to 25% for luxury autos selling for prices in excess of $100,000.

By shifting some of the tax burden on to an added cost of goods made in other countries, instead of as an added cost of goods made here, it would tend to make American made goods more competitive, and would be a boost for the American economy.

The sales tax could not provide sufficient revenues to meet the government's entire needs and an income tax would still be required. But we could create an exemption of, say, $60,000 for individuals, $120,000 for couples, and for anyone with income below that level there would be no withholding tax, and they would not even file a tax return. This is not a new concept, but was the original purpose of the exemption in the early years after the 16th amendment was passed in 1913 establishing the Federal Income Tax. These exemptions would totally eliminate the income tax for some 90% of American earners. For those 90% the concepts of "pre-tax" or "after-tax" deductions, and all of the complexities of "pre-tax" and "after-tax" savings programs like IRAs and 401Ks would become moot. All money saved would be tax free, and would only be taxed by incurring the sales tax when the money is spent. Other social engineering concepts that have been built into the income tax, such as whether to rent a home or to buy it, would cease to be influenced by tax considerations, and would be made purely based on preference and economic considerations. Is social engineering really a good purpose of the income tax? Can Congress really discern what personal behaviors are desirable and legislate it trough the income tax?

Those with incomes above the exempt level tend to be more sophisticated economically, and better equipped to deal with the intricacies of an income tax. Although with the high level of exemption, we could probably do away with many of those intricacies. Tax rates for income above the exempt level would be progressive, starting at, perhaps, 25%, and graduating to, perhaps, 50% for taxable income amounts above $1,000,000. With only 10% of us still filing tax returns, it would leave a far more manageable number of returns to process, and a more manageable task to audit them to insure that they are properly reported, calculated, and paid.

It would be a matter then of balancing sales tax rates and income tax rates to create the amounts of revenues needed to balance with the budgeted government expenditures.

CHAPTER 14
MINIMUM WAGE

The concept of making poor working people wealthier has tremendous appeal. But, in fact, the "minimum wage law" is really a misnomer. It is really a "maximum wage law". It does not dictate that any employer must actually pay the "minimum wage" to anyone. It really dictates that below that amount is the maximum wage which an employer is not allowed to pay to an employee. A willing employer is forbidden to pay an amount below that to a potential employee who might be willing and anxious to have the job. When government attempts to mandate a higher wage for a position than that which the market place has determined it is worth, one of several things will happen:

1. The company may have had that position as a convenience, not as a necessity. It may be an extra person to help out, clean up, or run errands when needed. And that was fine as long as it didn't cost much. But at the higher wage, they may be able to simply do without the position. Or they may find that at the higher cost the customer may be willing to perform the task themselves. How many "pump boys" are still pumping

gasoline? Does your grocery still employ people to bag your groceries? – Many don't.

2. At the lower wage, the investment in machinery to automate the position may not have offered an attractive pay back. But at the higher wage it may. Whatever became of "pin boys" at the bowling alley? How many gas stations have fully automated car washes?

3. The company may have been considering producing that product, or providing that service, overseas. At the lower wage that was not cost justified, but at the higher wage it certainly is. How much of our consumer goods do we still produce in the United States? How many people in Bangalore are answering your customer service calls?

4. With the higher wage, if they can not automate the job or send it overseas, the company will need to raise the price of the product or service. Will it still sell? At the same volume? Or will the company need to cut back production or eliminate that product altogether and, of course, the job along with it?

5. Or perhaps none of the above will happen, and the job will continue to exist at the higher wage. But this was an entry level job, and was held by a kid with few skills and no experience. Now that it is a higher paying job, will it attract more qualified people? And will the kid trying to find a place to start his career be out of a job?

Also, although the conversation is all about people working for the "minimum wage", it should be self evident that they are not the only ones whose wages will change if a higher "minimum wage" is enacted. When the wages for the lowest level employees are increased, the companies can not leave the wages of everyone else where they were. If the new hire with no skills is now to have a pay increase from $5.25 per hour to $7 per hour, what do you do with the more skilled worker who has worked his way up to $6 per hour? He can't also get a raise to only $7, and fall back to making the same wage as the new hire with no experience. He will have to get $8. And the lead person who was making $8? He will have to get a raise to $10 per hour. And with all the hourly workers getting a major raise, is the Foreman supposed to get none? I was running a factory that had some minimum wage workers in 1971 when the "minimum wage" was $1.60 per hour. Over the next ten years, as the minimum wage more than doubled to $3.35 per hour, we would meet with union officials to discuss increases to the wage scale for all workers in the plant. The meetings were brief. All workers would get the same percentage wage increase as the increase in the "minimum wage". And we would increase our prices accordingly. And maybe it's just a coincidence that during that period we had galloping inflation, and by 1981 the purchasing power of the new minimum wage of $3.35 was less than the purchasing power of the old minimum wage of $1.60 had been ten years earlier. And then, in order to combat the soaring inflation, Paul Volker, Chairman of the Federal Reserve, decided to raise interest rates to the stratosphere, and induced a horrible recession throwing millions of people out of their jobs. The unemployment rate grew from less than 4% in 1970 to nearly 10% in 1982. Were the "minimum wage" workers better off?

But what about "No one can support a family making minimum wage"? They are not supposed to! Minimum wage is for entry level positions for people without job skills. These are the jobs for the kid who dropped out of high school and has no skills, and doesn't even have a recommendation from a former employer that he will show up every day and try hard. These are the jobs where he can get some work experience, learn that it is important to show up every day and try hard, maybe learn how to load a truck, stock a shelf, or perhaps that the canned goods go on the bottom of the sack and the eggs go on top. Maybe he'll decide that it will be worth the effort to go to night school, get the GED, or apply for an apprenticeship, and now he is armed with a resume and a recommendation from an employer. Of course no one can support a family making minimum wage! But if we close off the opportunity for entry level jobs, the other choice may be to live on welfare, or push drugs, or hold up liquor stores.

CHAPTER 15
AFFIRMATIVE ACTION

In the 1960s and before, there were tremendous societal assumptions as to which people could hold what jobs. Some jobs had a gender built into the job title, such as "Stewardess". And society had an image that a stewardess was a young attractive white woman, and it was presumed that the airline's customers would not accept anyone not meeting that image in that position. A "Congressman" clearly was a man. Particularly, most of the positions with the highest pay and highest respect were deemed fitting only for middle aged white Protestant men. The anchor for the evening news was Walter Cronkite. Marcus Welby, MD was the public perception of what a doctor looked like. Doctors, lawyers, judges, Congressmen all were middle aged white men.

Even as the Civil Rights Movement swept away the legal barriers that had prevented people of minority groups from having the same opportunities as others, social expectations continued to exclude minorities from educational opportunity, from career choices, and from advancement opportunity. And if society did not necessarily exclude them, employers were nevertheless reluctant to push the envelope. Perhaps the public will be offended seeing someone of the "wrong" gender, "wrong" race, or who just looks "wrong", in the position? Perhaps the other employees will not accept a boss of a different race or gender? So it was necessary to force companies to employ and to promote people from groups that had been excluded. It was necessary for schools to do the same.

But in the short term, "Affirmative Action" really creates the opposite of what it is intended to accomplish. The long term objective is that everyone should be treated the same regardless of race, religion, gender, or other group identities. But in the meantime "Affirmative Action" requires that everyone be put into a group category, and that everyone be treated differently depending on what pigeonhole we have put them in. To be sure that we have accomplished that purpose, we develop quotas (everyone denies it, but clearly that is what it is). A company, must have the right percentage of black people, women, handicapped people, etc., and must have them equally represented in all areas of skill, responsibility, and income. Schools must have a "balanced" student body. But favoritism for members of a minority group tends to perpetuate an attitude among other members of society, as well as among the members of that group itself, that they are inherently unable to compete on a level playing field. It tends to negate the accomplishments of members of the group who really are well qualified, and in some cases are quite exceptional. People question: "Did they get the position just because of their race or gender"?

So "Affirmative Action" was always intended to be a short term solution. It was a step to change the societal biases that precluded members of minority groups from having equal opportunities, and a step toward creating a "color blind" society, where people would be judged on their abilities, not on their group categorization. Today, there are people of every race, religion, gender, and every other group, serving in every position in business and in government. The most likely candidates for the next presidential election include a white woman and a black man. The evening news is likely to have a panel including men and women, black people, white people, Asian people, fat people, thin people, gay people, and any other category. If you watch a movie or TV drama, the doctors, judges, corporate leaders, are as likely to be a black woman as they are to be a white man. Oprah, a black woman, is one of the most influential people in our society, followed closely by Rosie, an openly gay woman. Men are Stewardesses and Hooters Girls. Girls are Shoeshine Boys. We have come a long way in the last few decades. Surprisingly, or perhaps not surprisingly, the only institutions that still maintain an open policy for bigotry and bias, for positions for which you need not apply if you are the wrong gender or gay, are some of our religious institutions. Yes, some of our religions still have a policy of keeping everyone in their place.

It may take another generation or two until those of us raised with old stereotypes die off, and our children and grandchildren replace us, and before bigotry and bias truly disappear. But the sooner we learn to judge everyone by their abilities and the "content of their character and not by the color of their skin", or by whatever other method we have devised for categorizing people, the better.

CHAPTER 16
WELFARE

The old saying is "give a poor person a fish you feed him for a day, teach him to fish you feed him for a lifetime". In our wealthy society, no one should starve. However, we should not be giving out handouts to people sitting around doing nothing. It is not good for society, and it is not good for them. We need to set up job training schools aimed at making people employable, and anyone requiring government to support them, should be required to attend a school in order to receive the payments. School counselors should meet with the individuals to identify what jobs suit their aptitudes and interests, and what education and training will enable them to qualify for a position. It may require teaching them to speak, read, or write the English language, or basic arithmetic. It may be specific job training – whether that involves learning to flip burgers, work a cash register, building trades, cutting hair, or any other job where people can become employable. The schools should include job placement counselors. Bus service will need to be part of the program. But no able bodied person should be allowed to make a life-style choice of sitting around doing nothing and being supported by the government.

There is, of course, a high proportion of single mothers who are unemployed and require welfare assistance to sustain them. The story is that they can not have a job because of the need to care for the children. Nor can they attend a job training school. What is needed is affordable day care centers for the children so that the mothers can be employed or go to job training school. In addition to allowing the parent to be employed or to attend school, the day care centers would insure that the children would receive adequate nutrition, medical check-ups, inoculations, and a stimulating environment. The day care centers themselves can become a substantial employer of single mothers.

Although these programs will be expensive, they will be the best investment we can make. The pay back will be not only that welfare will not be an endless money pit, but in human terms, what can be better than helping people to become self supporting and self reliant?

But for those who due to physical, mental, or emotional disabilities are truly incapable of doing productive work, there needs to be a provision for them. In a compassionate society with our great wealth, no one should need to live in a cardboard box, hover over a steam vent, or beg on the street. Private and religious charities do a wonderful job of providing shelters, but government should be helping to adequately fund them, or operate government run shelters that would ensure that every person has a place to go with a roof over their head, washroom facilities, suitable clothing, nutritious food, and basic medical attention, and a means to get there.

CHAPTER 17
NATIONAL ID CARD

Our primary means of identification is a state issued driver's license, with no ready means to even verify that it is real. And what underage kid has never figured out how easy it is to fake it. If you want to make a profession of creating fake documents, this one is a piece of cake. Particularly, in that the driver's license may be issued by any of fifty states, and the person viewing it may be utterly unfamiliar with what a driver's license from that state looks like. This is the document that verifies that it is you who is getting on the airplane. It is you cashing the check or charging thousands of dollars to the credit card. It is you applying for a job. It is you applying for the loan. For international travel we use a passport with technology that was last updated when we unhitched the horse from the horseless carriage.

In the meantime, we have lists of people we consider to be too dangerous to allow on an airplane, but no real means of identifying who is getting on. We have an enormous problem with identity theft: people using credit cards that do not belong to them, taking out loans under names that are not theirs, or buying property and taking out mortgage loans under false names, before disappearing. We can not control the vast flow of people entering our country without authorization, who are then able to get a job, presenting false identity documents and false social security numbers. They are able to enroll their children in our public schools and apply for public aid.

We could easily issue ID cards with a magnetic stripe that would tie into a computer data base and verify that the card is real. The credit card companies have had the ability anywhere in the world to scan a card and read the data encoded on the magnetic stripe for decades. Add to it a fingerprint for identification (a technology currently in use at my grocery store) and we could actually know that the rightful owner of the card is the person presenting it. The computer does not really have to compare the fingerprint with millions of others, but only check a few points in order to verify that the encoded identification matches the identification in the computer. Because the data is in the computer data base, not just on the card, this system could be made virtually impossible to falsify. The National ID card would replace the birth certificate, the Social Security card, the Voter's Registration Card, and the passport. Like driver's licenses and passports, they would be renewed every few years. The computer would be programmed to look for anomalies that would indicate possible falsification, such as the use of a card with the identity of someone who had previously been reported as deceased, or use of a card for someone holding multiple jobs in different parts of the country, or holding several full time jobs simultaneously.

It would be invaluable for identifying who is a citizen eligible to vote and for recording that they voted only once in an election and not several times (yes, even in Chicago). We could identify who is really getting on the airplane, who really is applying for a loan, who is using the credit card, and a myriad of other applications. It would be a major tool in tracking fugitives or people failing to make payments on government loans, failing to pay income taxes, or failing to make court ordered child support payments.

It also could be a tool to replace the arduous task of census taking, with far more accurate results, and with the ability to reliably and easily compile demographic data. The computer data base would have a real time record of every citizen, every resident alien, every authorized temporary resident student or temporary worker, and every visitor. The data base would have information on age, gender, where people live, how they are employed, and any other characteristics that were deemed useful.

First time visitors to the U.S. would be required to get an ID card as part of the visa process. It would be scanned at every port of entry, and checked for "undesirables", and would track the purpose of the visit, permitted activities (vacation, business, student, employment), and permitted duration of stay. It would be checked again at every port of debarkation. The computer would flag anyone who had overstayed their permitted visit.

Yes, there is tremendous resistance to providing information to allow the government to track your activities and movements because of the sinister Orwellian overtones. But the government already does have all of this information! The IRS and the Social Security Administration do know where you live and where you work, your address, your phone number and, if you are one of the millions who file taxes electronically, even your e-mail address and bank account number. You already give your name and present identification every time you travel by plane. The phone company has a record of every call you make. The bank and the credit card companies have a record of every transaction. The difference would be that with a National ID Card, it could be verified that the information attributed to you was in fact actually you.

CHAPTER 18
IMMIGRATION

There are an estimated twelve million people currently living in the US without authorization, and it is our own fault for utterly ignoring the situation for the past twenty years. They have every reason to believe that we haven't cared. We have allowed them to live in the U.S., to earn wages, to buy property, to send their kids to public schools. They have married (some to U.S. citizens), and their children are now U.S. citizens. To start deporting them now would be unfair and cruel to them and disruptive to their communities and to the businesses where they work. We had a General Amnesty in 1986 (Immigration Reform and Control Act - Simpson-Mazzoli Act (IRCA), Pub. L. No. 99-603, 100 Stat. 3359, Nov. 6, 1986). We must once again have a general amnesty, and announce a new policy to prevent a repetition in another twenty years. It certainly sounds like déjà vu all over again, but it doesn't need to be.

We can build fences and post armies along borders, but to what purpose? There are millions of foreigners crossing our borders legally every day – visitors, vacationers, businessmen, students, temporary workers, and others who are not authorized to reside here long term. Why does anyone need to sneak across? The obvious way to control illegal immigration is to truly make it impossible for unauthorized persons to get a job, to go to school, to send their kids to school, or to access government services. For that, it is necessary to have a National ID Card that accesses a national data bank, and cannot be forged. We need penalties for hiring people without proper authorization stiff enough that no employer would do so – even those employing a maid or a nanny could be required to notify the national data bank. And we actually need to enforce those laws 100% of the time, not on a few random and serendipitous raids. Redirect a portion of the funds being spent on posting an army along the border to actually policing U.S. employers. And spend some of those funds to publicize in foreign nations that we have truly made it impossible for people entering the U.S. without proper authorization to find employment, or otherwise to make a life here.

Of course, the majority of the people who come to live and work in the United States without authorization are coming from Mexico. There is no flood of illegal immigrants coming from Canada, with a border equally long – they are happy to live in Canada. So why aren't Mexicans happy to live in Mexico? Mexico is a lovely country, with a great climate, natural beauty, thousands of miles of coastline, resources, rich culture, and an ethic of education and hard work. And yet, somehow, there simply are not sufficient opportunities for Mexicans to earn a living in Mexico. They are not coming here because they prefer our culture - they don't. They come solely for economic opportunity that they can not find at home. Surely, the real answer to the problem of Mexicans flooding into the U.S. to work is to find ways to help Mexico develop their economy.

It brings up, of course, the question as to why is the economy of the United States so strong? We have long been innovators, and the consummate entrepreneurs. But perhaps more importantly, we are also consummate consumers. The insatiable appetite of Americans for consumer goods and services is the engine that propels the U.S. economy, and the economies of many other developed and developing countries which have economies based on supplying American consumers. Much of the credit for creating the American consumer has always been given to Henry Ford. A hundred years ago, he realized that if he would pay his factory workers a higher wage that they could then become customers for his products. It worked. And ever since, America has been a land with an enormous middle class, producing with great efficiency, earning high wages, and consuming voraciously. But today, perhaps the real engine that drives the American economy is easy credit. Easy credit is obviously a two edged sword. It can bring economic ruin to those who use it unwisely, and to the institutions who grant it unwisely. But if used properly, it allows Americans to buy everything first, and pay later. We start with the education, running up massive student loan debt, while preparing for a high paying career. And then we buy the big house with the big mortgage, and the big car with the big payment book, and put everything we might desire on the credit card, all to be paid for later. No wonder we are able to keep on consuming, we don't have to wait until we have earned the money to pay for anything. But buying now and paying later creates the demand for goods and services that keeps us employed, so that we can make the payments. And America, which has virtually gone out of the business of producing consumer goods, nevertheless continues to enjoy minimal unemployment and great wealth.

So why doesn't that work for Mexico? I don't know. I'm not sure that anyone knows. When Mexicans come to the U.S, they are certainly hard working and highly productive. Mexicans certainly have the propensity for producing and consuming. I was recently in Puerto Vallarta, which I have visited from time to time over the past thirty five years. It is, obviously, not typical of all of Mexico. As a major tourist destination, it has had an enormous influx of money for many years, and has created a large population of fairly wealthy people. Currently, there is a tremendous amount of additional resort construction going on, but equally there is booming construction of housing. There are crews on top of houses everywhere you look. Lovely neighborhoods reminiscent of affluent communities in suburban U.S.A. Walking through a neighborhood, my wife and I came to a place where we could see a line of cars ahead parked along the street. That's unusual! But, on arriving alongside the cars, we noticed that they were mostly SUVs and Minivans, each with a woman with great hair and make-up, and talking on a cell phone. I've certainly seen this scene before, just not in Mexico. I said "they're waiting to pick up the kids from school". And sure enough, two blocks later, the school was just letting out. A scene right out of the suburbs of North Shore Chicago. To go with these communities are shopping malls with way-up-scale department stores. All it took was a massive infusion of consumer spending and of capital.

We have helped to create thriving economies in Japan, Taiwan, Korea, Germany and other countries of the world. Surely working together with the government of Mexico, we can find ways to create a boom in the economy of Mexico. Spending money to create economic development in Mexico makes vastly more sense than spending it to build fences along the border or to pay for an army to patrol the border. If we need to subsidize U.S. businesses to build plants and run production in Mexico rather than half way around the world, isn't that the same money we would spend dealing with the problems of having twelve million unauthorized immigrants living here? Wouldn't we make the world a better place for the people of the United States, and for the people of Mexico, investing in creating economic opportunity in Mexico, rather than in ways to keep Mexicans out of the U.S.?

CHAPTER 19
CONSERVATIVE / LIBERAL

Highly publicized opinions today tend to be divided into two categories: Liberal and Conservative. The Left and the Right.

There are numerous articles and books in which Conservatives and Liberals berate each other. Remarkably, the authors invariably fail to define their terms. They ramble on railing against this or that person of the opposite bent, without addressing: what is a Conservative or a Liberal? What are the positions that each embraces? What is the underlying philosophy behind those differences of opinion?

Who is it that has decided that all people, each with an entire range of opinions on a multitude of subjects, should be neatly divided into just two categories? Is it the politicians, who can then label their opponent with a derogatory epithet? "He is a bleeding heart tax and spend liberal". "He is a military industrial complex conservative".

Or is it the news media, because one-word labels make for easy headlines. And it makes it much easier to identify a person "John

Doe the Conservative" or "The Liberal Mary Smith", than it would be to actually address the person's views on various issues.

Or is it us? Are we two lazy to delve into actual positions and arguments on issues, and is it easier to simply slap a label on people, and form a judgment of them based on the label?

The dictionary definitions (The American Heritage® Dictionary of the English Language, Fourth Edition, Copyright © 2000 by Houghton Mifflin Company) are simple:

A Conservative is one "Favoring traditional views and values; tending to oppose change; conforming to the standards and conventions of the middle class". "Bourgeois, cautious, constant, controlled, conventional, old guard, orthodox, traditionalistic".

A Liberal is one "Favoring proposals for reform, open to new ideas for progress, and tolerant of the ideas and behavior of others". "Broad-minded, progressive, avant-garde, enlightened, flexible, humanitarian, indulgent, lenient, libertarian, permissive, receptive, reformist, tolerant"

Thus, the traditional Conservative is a rugged individualist. The man is the master of his domain. He is responsible for providing the family with food, clothing and shelter, protecting them, and leading them. He runs his business without requiring help, and without interference, from government. He believes in laissez faire free enterprise. Save for a rainy day, and for old age, and take care of yourself and your family. The woman is his helpmate. Her role is to have, to nurture, and to rear children, and to maintain the household. The role of government is to do those tasks that only a government can do - provide for the common defense, make treaties with other nations, provide police, courts and prisons, and public works. The Conservative believes that the least Government is the best Government.

The classic Liberal recognizes that there are things the conservative approach does not adequately address. Unregulated businesses may spread pollutants in the air, the water, and the earth. They may chop down the forests, and lay the earth open in pursuit of minerals. They may be abusive of their employees, forcing child labor, excessive hours, poor pay, and unsafe conditions. They may form trusts and monopolies, creating enormous wealth for the owners, while providing inferior products at high prices to the public. Also, there are some people who are not able to satisfactorily cope in an unregulated competitive free enterprise system. Perhaps because they are a member of a downtrodden minority or the victim of bias and prejudice. Or perhaps they are women who do not want to be a "helpmate". Or perhaps they have failed to adequately provide for illness or old age. Or perhaps they are not as big, as strong, as smart, as ambitious, or as well educated as others. Or perhaps, they simply didn't have the foresight to be born to rich and powerful parents. For all these reasons, the Liberal sees a more active role for Government to be involved with society.

But then there is a third group, that is neither the Rugged Individualist Conservative, nor the Caring Liberal. They are people of "Faith" who are guided by "Dogma". The dictionary defines faith as "Belief that does not rest on logical proof or material evidence", and Dogma as "Characterized by an authoritative, arrogant assertion of unproved or unprovable principles.... dictatorial." Their arguments for their positions on any subject are to cite chapter and verse, to quote an authority figure, and there is no room for logic, discussion nor debate.

Surprisingly, for people who profess to be deeply religious, they tend to be unaccepting and unforgiving of those who are different from them. On a biking trip in the Tetons, we became quite friendly with another couple. One evening after dinner we were sitting around talking when our friend said: "You're such nice people, it's a shame that you are going to hell". Judy said: "excuse me?" And he replied, "Yes, it doesn't matter that you're nice people. You haven't accepted Jesus as your Savior, and so you are going to hell!"

Also surprisingly, for those who profess awe for the Creator, they tend to be anti-science, preferring biblical explanations for natural phenomenon rather than actual observation of God's works. In the words of Galileo Galilei, the 16th century astronomer "I do not feel obliged to believe that the same God who has endowed us with sense, reason and intellect has intended us to forgo their use". He was then tried by the Inquisition for the heresy of pointing out that the earth revolves around the sun, and sentenced to confinement for the rest of his life.

Although they would seem to be polar opposites, the Rugged Individualists and the Dogmatists have somehow melded into a single group, which today is considered the Conservatives, the Right Wing, the Red States, and has become the Republican Party. It hasn't always been so.

It was a Republican, Abe Lincoln, who believed in the authority of a strong central government that could override the authority of the states. It was Abe who presided over a "great civil war testing whether that Nation or any nation so conceived and so dedicated to the proposition that all men are created equal, could long endure". It was Abe who proclaimed that the government of the United States of America could forbid the individual states to have laws allowing people to be held as property in servitude, and he set the slaves free.

It was a Republican, Teddy Roosevelt, who was known as the trust busting regulator of monopolistic businesses. It was Teddy who promoted trade unions to fight for fair treatment of the workers. And who built the canal in Panama, and sent the Great White Fleet to spread the influence of the United States throughout the world. It was Teddy who formed the Progressive (Bullmoose) Party.

More recently, Barry Goldwater, the father of the modern conservative movement in the Republican Party, was a libertarian. He wrote in a 1994 Washington Post essay "I am a conservative Republican, but I believe in Democracy and the separation of church and state. The conservative movement is founded on the simple tenet that people have the right to live life as they please as long as they don't hurt anyone else in the process." He was a supporter of a woman's right to choose whether or not to have a baby, and an ardent supporter of the rights of gay people to live without suffering bias and discrimination from society. He was distressed as Jerry Falwell's "Moral Majority" made inroads into the Republican Party and they sought to impose their views into government. He is famously quoted as saying: "Every good Christian should line up and kick Jerry Falwell's ass."

The influence of the religious right has so permeated the Republican Party that true Conservatives would no longer recognize it.

CHAPTER 20
FRAMING

There are a number of coded words and phrases that do not at all mean what they would seem to mean. Many of these get picked up by the media and are used so much that we start believing that they have the meaning intended while at the same time carrying the hidden message of the normal meanings of the words.

For instance: "Pro-Life". It sounds like people who simply love life. Anyone who is not "Pro-Life" must be "Anti-Life" or "Pro-Death". Therefore "Pro-Life" people are clearly right and good and any one disagreeing with them must be wrong and evil. The "Pro-Life" people and the media have so managed to incorporate this phrase into our vernacular that even Bill Maher uses it when referring to these people. But in fact, we have all come to understand that this phrase actually has nothing at all to do with describing people with a greater love of life than others. It really refers to people with a belief that government should force all women who become pregnant to have babies even if they desperately do not want to do so – criminalizing them and anyone who assists them in terminating a pregnancy and throwing them into prisons. Some of these are people who would bomb clinics and murder the doctors and nurses inside. They have no love of life, but only a compulsion to force their will upon others.

Another is: "Family Values". Sounds wonderful! Who is not in favor of families, and values? Anyone who disagrees with the proponents of "Family Values" must hate families, have no values, and be morally bankrupt and evil. Of course, the phrase actually has nothing to do with who it is that loves families or has values. It is code for bigots who hate most anyone who isn't just like them – like the white zealots who in former years were proud members of the Klan. They hate gay people, black people, Jews, and want to deprive the rest of us of our rights to live life as we see fit. They seek to impose their concept of "proper behavior" upon all.

There is of course also the "No Child Left Behind" Act. Who would want to leave any child behind? But the Act focuses far more on more standardized testing and more administration, and far less time that the children's behinds are in the classroom.

And the "Patriot Act". In fact, it is just an acronym for an act "Providing Appropriate Tools Required to Intercept and Obstruct Terrorism", and has nothing to do with Patriotism. It actually has to do with empowering the Government to ignore the Bill of Rights, a document fundamental to "The American Way". It allows the Government to conduct illegal searches and seizures and to ignore the rights of the accused to be considered innocent until proven guilty. As Ben Franklin the father of American patriotism said: "Those who would give up Essential Liberty to purchase a little Temporary Safety, deserve neither Liberty nor Safety."

How about "The Moral Majority"? Who could argue with those people? Of course, they were not a majority, and certainly were not moral. They were plagued with infighting, scandals, and criminal indictments.

Then there is "The Death Tax". That certainly sounds like something you should oppose. But it used to be called the Estate Tax - a tax that meant the children of millionaires would get a few less millions of dollars when their rich daddies died, instead of having to take more money from hard working people struggling to eke out a living. But that is only if you believe that someone has to pay the bills for government's expenditures. What if we don't take the money from the millionaire heirs, and we don't take it from anyone? And that brings us to:

"Tax Relief". Doesn't that sound wonderful? We are all relieved from the cruel burdens of taxation! But who pays the bills? If reduced taxes are not matched by reduced expenditures, all we are doing is not paying the bills. We still owe the money; we're just not paying it. We're just piling up more and more debt. How is that "relief"?

Another example that has been widely used and abused is the term "War on ...." We have had the "War on Poverty", the continuing "War on Drugs", and now the "War on Terror". Real wars, for all their horrors, have well defined enemies, well defined objectives, and after a year or two, sometimes a little longer, sometimes much shorter, come to well defined conclusions. Either one side is victorious and the other surrenders or both sides recognize that the war is a disaster, and they come to a truce. These artificial "Wars on ...." allow their framers to talk about them as if they were real wars. We must "Stay the Course". "We will achieve Victory! " In these pseudo wars, we cannot even define what an event that would constitute victory would look like. But being "At War" justifies whatever actions, whatever expenses, and whatever sacrifices we are asked to make.

For the media to throw these terms around as if they meant what they seem to mean, without qualifying them in quote marks, or as the "so called ...." is lazy, disingenuous, and contrary to the duty of the media to present fair and balanced news.

CHAPTER 21
EVOLUTION & SCIENTIFIC METHOD

For all the talk about "Intelligent Design", I am unable to find any clear definition of what it means. The discourse usually talks about "teaching the controversy" and that somehow "Intelligent Design" is an alternative to the evolution of the species. And yet, I have never found anything in "Intelligent Design" to explain: if living things did not evolve, how did the myriad variety of living things come to exist in their present forms? At least with "Creationism", there was an explanation – God created all living things in their present forms in seven days and plopped them down on planet Earth. I have no problem accepting that the design of the universe, the Earth, and of the living things that inhabit Earth, is extraordinarily complex and that it exhibits an incredible intelligence that is, in fact, far beyond our ability to comprehend. But what is "the controversy"? Yes, the Creator designed living things to evolve.

Some point out that Science does not have all of the answers. They are right, of course. Science does not have all of the answers. With regard to living things, we are missing knowledge of the most basic thing – that is, how did the first living things come into existence? Did that happen once, and all living things since have evolved from that first living cell? Or, did it happen many times? And are the living things currently in existence derived from different original life? Are living things still coming into existence from non-living things? And if not, why not?

But, of course, that is what Science is all about. No Scientist claims to have all the answers, or that the answers we do have, are infallible. As brilliant as Newton's Law of Motion F=MA and law of Gravity $G=(M_1 \times M_2) \div D^2$ were, they were modified by Einstein. Science is not about having infallible answers, but is a method of searching for answers. Using observation, experimentation, and reason, to derive hypothesis as to how natural phenomena are structured and how things work. And then subjecting those hypotheses to repeated testing and retesting, to demonstrate unvarying repeatability, until we accept them as scientific theories.

When people talk of "Miracles", they are referring to things that occurred that defied the Laws of Nature. In fact, of course, the real Miracle is that the Creator structured the Universe, the Earth, and the living things that inhabit the Earth, so well that there are no exceptions to Natural Law. The real Miracle is that there are no Miracles! That is how we are able to have Science. If the structure of things were sometimes given to varying whimsically, if effects did not invariably follow causes, there could be no Science. We certainly are far from having all the answers, but we know that things are structured, they are constant, and we can continue our search to understand the world and the universe in which we live.

Another area where "People of Faith" are conflicted with science is in some areas of medical research. For instance: I have no idea what will be accomplished through research on embryonic stem cells, nor what will be accomplished by research on other types of stem cells, nor what will be accomplished in other areas of medical research. No one really does – if we already knew the answers, we wouldn't need to do research. Certainly embryonic stem cell research needs to compete with all other medical research for budget dollars to be allocated to it. Those budget dollars should be allocated by people knowledgeable in the field based on their assessment of likely short term and long term benefits to human kind.

But if there is an area of medical research that most knowledge-able people in the field believe to have the potential for curing afflictions that are devastating to millions of people, why would any one want to single out that area of research, and prevent it? What horrible people these must be, to put some vague concept regarding the sacrosanct rights of a collection of cells in a Petri dish ahead of the well-being of their fellow man?

These people have other areas of medical research that also bring up "moral issues" for them.

Research into the processes by which life is created is fraught with such "moral issues". When it was demonstrated that Dolly the Sheep could be created through cloning, thereby bypassing the normal method of creating offspring, they went into a tizzy. They began conjuring up all the ways in which this knowledge might be abused. Cloning people in order to harvest their organs! Cloning armies of super soldiers!

Yes, knowledge can be the undoing of mankind. We certainly have been beset by the knowledge we have gained since the dawn of civilization in creating better and more effective ways of killing each other. From the time the first man tied a piece of flint onto the end of a stick to make a better spear, and then to make a bow and shoot an arrow, and then to make gunpowder and guns, and cannons, and bombs. And when Einstein discovered that a tiny amount of matter could be converted into an enormous amount of energy, the first thing that was done with that knowledge was to make a vastly more powerful bomb!

But is the answer to squelch research? To stick our heads in the sand? To revel in ignorance? Is, in fact, ignorance bliss? Is the salvation of humankind to avoid learning, to avoid knowledge, and to keep ourselves stupid?

Or can we learn to have knowledge, and learn to use it wisely and judiciously, for the benefit of ourselves, and for the benefit of the planet Earth, and all of its human and non-human inhabitants?

CHAPTER 22
GAY MARRIAGE / GAY RIGHTS

Aren't the people who oppose Gay Marriage the same people who used to want to make it a felony for people of different races to be married or to engage in sex? And didn't they criminalize any other type of sex but the kinds they approve? Sodomy laws and misogyny laws have only recently disappeared. And is there no one left for them to hate except gays?

It is not a matter of whether or not you or I like or approve of gay behavior. It is a matter of accepting the rights of others to live their lives as they see fit. It gets back to the question of whether the rights of men are endowed by the Creator, and the rights of Government are granted by consent of the governed. Or, do all our rights belong to the government, to be bestowed upon us only if our actions conform to the common sense of morality. If we allow discrimination for any type of behavior which is not to our liking, aren't we all going to find people who do not like some part of what we do?

There are many people who do many things that I don't relate to, and can't imagine why they would want to do them. My brother-in-Law would be delighted to sit through an entire performance of Wagner's Ring Trilogy Operas – to me it sounds like unimaginable torture. But the point is, I don't have to like it, and I don't have to do it. He gets to do what he wants to do, I get to do what I want to do, and what he does really doesn't affect me.

But then there is the argument that homosexuality is an "abomination". God abhors this deviant behavior. But isn't it God who has created people who are homosexual! What kind of people set themselves up to judge their fellow man based on "knowing what God abhors"? Or are they judging God? You would have to be incredibly self-important to believe that you have been appointed to know and to enforce God's will. But isn't that contrary to the tenets of religion? Is it not only "He that is without sin among you, let him first cast a stone"? "Judge not, lest ye be judged"?

But, to be fair, perhaps it is not quite that simple. We do, and should of course, have laws regulating things which we are not permitted to do. There properly are laws forbidding us to do things when what we do has direct adverse physical affects on others. We are not permitted to attack another person or to steal their property.

But there are also laws prohibiting behavior that does not have a direct physical affect on others. We are not permitted to do things on our own property or on public property that would interfere with another's "quiet enjoyment" of their own property. So the concept of a law banning activity that does not have a direct physical affect on another does, and should, exist. But is the mere knowledge that someone is behaving in a manner that offends you reason enough to have a law to prevent that behavior? Are there behaviors that are so universally offensive that they should not be permitted? And who is to decide? When does the right of one person to not be offended justify forbidding another to lead his life as he sees fit?

The other argument for making gay marriage illegal is that it destroys the "Institution of Marriage". What is "The institution of Marriage?" and what does a marriage between two gay people have to do with it? Is the implication that the vows of marriage are made vastly more important than they otherwise would be because of thousands of years of history and tradition in which humankind has always held those vows to be sacrosanct? That the vow to love each other until "death do us part" has throughout human history been treated with such respect that "no man may put asunder that which God has joined together"? And that the greatest threat to the sanctity of those unions would be a loving same sex couple wishing to pledge to join their lives together? This notwithstanding the fact that nearly half of heterosexual marriages are ending in divorce. Or the long tradition of couples living together for decades while detesting each other. Or societies where having multiple wives is common, and where twelve year old daughters are given in marriage to old men. Or the long tradition of keeping mistresses and lovers on the side. Or an occasional King having his Queen beheaded in order to get rid of her. And a loving marriage between two people of the same sex is what is going to destroy the institution of marriage? Boy! Talk about a stretch in inventing justification for one's bigotry and bias!

CHAPTER 23
ABORTION

What kind of people would want to force women to have babies when they desperately do not want to do so? Having unwanted babies is a disaster for the mother, the baby, and for society. If it is really about "rights of a fetus", why make exceptions for rape & incest? What has the manner of conception got to do with fetal rights? If they want to prevent abortions, why do the same people oppose sex education and contraception? Or is it about "punishing" women for having sex except for the purpose of procreation? Do these people really see a baby as a "punishment?

And is that why these people even tried to block the "Plan B" pill being made readily available over-the-counter. Are they afraid that people will not be "punished" for having sex? One would think that if there is anything that we all could agree on, it would be that if an unwanted pregnancy can be avoided, we should certainly want to do so.

No one has ever wanted to have an abortion. There are no "pro-abortion" people. Nor are there any "anti-life" people. But sometimes aborting an unwanted pregnancy or a pregnancy where there are severe medical problems with the fetus or for the woman carrying it becomes a compelling course of action for a pregnant woman. The argument has become charged with emotion. Even the word "abortion" has become charged with emotion. But living in a free society requires that we "judge not". There are many things that each of us do that others strongly disagree with. But do we really want government imposing our moral values on others, and having them impose their moral values on us.

Does "Life begin at Conception"? Is terminating a pregnancy "Baby Killing"? At conception, is there a new "person" with rights that supersede the rights of the woman in whose body it resides? Does society have a responsibility to protect the rights of the new "person"? The fact is that the question of when is there a new "person" is one of those questions which simply does not have a "right" answer. Intelligent, reasonable people could discuss the subject forever, and never reach a conclusive answer. Like the question of "how many trees does it take to make a forest?" It is really a question of definition, not of facts. We all know the facts. A sperm can combine with an ovum, which can then become a fertilized ovum, which can then become an embryo, which then can become a fetus, which then can become a baby. Do we have an obligation to protect the "right to life" of every potential new person?

Clearly, there are an unlimited number of potential new persons. Every ovum is capable of combining with every sperm to produce a new person. Do we abrogate our responsibility to the "right to life" of a new person if we fail to copulate at every possible moment? The creation of a new "person" is a process. When that new person has "rights" is a matter for society to select a measurable time, as it does with other "rights" for people. Traditionally, government has recognized a "new person" when that person is born. That is when the census bureau counts a new person. That is when the IRS recognizes a new dependent person.

It is the time elapsed from the time of birth that other rights and obligations accrue – the obligation of the parents to provide formal education, the right to drive an automobile, the right to enter into contracts, vote, serve in the military, or buy liquor and tobacco. It is also the time when the rights of the baby no longer are physically tied to the rights of the mother.

Is "Life" sacred? I certainly agree that I consider my life, your life, and the lives of those I know and love, to be sacred. But is the concept of "Life" sacred? Did the Creator intend that every living being would survive? We know it isn't so! He has designed all living things to create far more progeny than will survive. Insects and fish produce hundreds, or thousands, of offspring at a time. Very few survive. Even most mammals, who produce relatively few offspring at a time, would still rapidly overpopulate their environments, but nature is designed that the smallest, the weakest, the least fit, will not survive, and the species will evolve and improve. Humans, who generally produce only one baby at a time, with a very long period of gestation and infancy, still are capable of producing as many as twenty offspring from a single mother. Historically, many would die from pestilence, war, and famine before they reached an age to reproduce themselves. No, nature does not consider "Life" to be sacred, but actually considers life to be quite expendable. Surprisingly, most of the people who are most adamant about the "Sanctity of Life" also consider living things to be expendable. They are not the ones who are vegetarians. Vegetarians are "Effete Liberals". Good red blooded Conservative Americans love to eat good red meat, and are not concerned with the billions of cows, sheep, pigs, chickens, and other animals that we slaughter each year to feed ourselves. They are also the people who are strong advocates of the right to keep guns, and are willing to sacrifice the twenty thousand Americans who are murdered by guns each year. And they love to go hunting with their guns, and shoot God's creatures. They are also the strongest advocates for executing criminals. And for keeping a strong military so that we don't need to exercise diplomacy when dealing with our enemies, but can bomb them into submission. Apparently they only consider that "Life is Sacred " when they wish to impose their will upon others.

And what about those who say "I sure am glad that my parents didn't abort me". But you might also say "I sure am glad that my mom didn't have a 'headache' the night I was conceived". Or, "I sure am glad that my parents went out and got drunk and horny the night I was conceived". The fact is, that you are an accident, we all are. The unique set of genes in your make-up came from two people who were not considering genealogy at the time they met. And they copulated, not necessarily with the intention of procreating, but perhaps out of nothing but lust. In fact, if you consider yourself to have been a candidate for a terminated pregnancy, they quite likely were not intending to produce an offspring. But whether they were or were not, people have sex many times without creating a pregnancy. And when a pregnancy does occur, about fifty percent of the time Nature aborts the pregnancy - miscarriages are that common, usually early in the pregnancy, frequently before the woman even knows she is pregnant. But assuming that all of that works out, and you were born, your particular make-up came from out of their gene pool, and the set of genes passed on to you were chosen by Nature, who randomly discarded half of what was available, and kept the other half. We certainly know that siblings with the same potential gene pool can be radically different. Yes, you are happy to be alive, but the fact is that there are millions of reasons why the particular person you are, with the particular set of genes and characteristics that define you, might never have come into being.

Other nations do not have this obsession with banning abortion. Most all nations in Europe freely allow a pregnancy to be terminated through the first trimester. Even highly Catholic Portugal just passed legislation, following a referendum, allowing abortions through the first ten weeks of pregnancy. This was enacted by their Parliament (and did not need not to be dictated by their courts), because their legislature actually deals with issues, and is not busy deciding by what name to call fried potatoes.

If we are looking for a compromise position, setting a time limit on how far into pregnancy a legal abortion could be performed without there being a medical necessity would be a reasonable compromise. That would deal with the vast majority of situations. And later term abortions required due to medical needs might require a doctor to certify the need for the abortion and receive approval from a panel of doctors, if such a mechanism could be established without being too cumbersome and time consuming to work. Like all compromises, this one would be equally hated by both sides. The radical anti-abortionists, who are certain that a fertilized egg is a baby, would still be incensed about "baby killing". The radical free choice people will still be incensed with any infringement by government upon a woman's free choice. But life is full of compromises, and compromise is the way people with diametrically opposed opinions resolve them peacefully.

This would still leave issues such as whether a pregnant minor requires permission from a parent (or must notify a parent) before terminating a pregnancy. In theory, we would all agree that our minor children should not be undergoing any medical procedure without our being involved. But, in fact, it is the people who are most adamant about requiring parental approval who are most likely to severely beat their daughter if she tells them that she is pregnant, or to force a disastrous marriage between two kids, or to force her to have the baby to "teach her a lesson".

CHAPTER 24
"WAR ON TERROR"

Three million Americans will die this year. Thirty thousand will be brutally murdered. Forty thousand crushed on the highways. Thousands more will die in tragic accidents in their homes, while pursuing pastimes, or in accidents in the workplace. Hundreds of thousands of young people will die torturous deaths from hideous diseases. So why do we make headlines when people are killed by fanatics with some obscure political agenda? Why are those deaths "TERROR" and most of the other deaths scarcely get a paragraph on the third page? And isn't publicity exactly what these fanatics want? Isn't it our Government, and those who manage the news media, the ones who are creating "TERROR", and encouraging "TERRORISTS" through their inordinate publicity of these people's activities, and their obsession with the subject?

This is not to say that we shouldn't be taking measures to prevent fanatics from killing us – we should! And we should devote enormous resources toward doing so. But we devote enormous resources toward trying to prevent deaths from other causes. We employ millions of people and spend hundreds of billions of dollars on police, courts, and prisons to protect us from criminals.

We also have a multitude of automotive engineers to improve auto safety and highway engineers to create safer roads to protect us from traffic carnage. There are millions of firemen, workplace safety inspectors, and emergency medical personnel to protect us from trauma at home, at play, and at work. We spend hundreds of billions of dollars on medical research, hospitals, doctors, nurses and other medical personnel and medications and treatments to protect us from the ravages of disease. All of this is done without screaming headlines dominating the news on a daily basis. Do we really want to be obsessed with these fanatics with their obscure political agendas?

And the problem with the obsession with "terrorism" is that it leads to some responses that are horrible, and horribly counterproductive.

So that our politicians could show us that they were "doing something" about "terrorism", in spite of the objections of all of our traditional friends and allies and the world community, our government decided to invade Iraq. In Iraq, we have killed and maimed tens of thousands of people, and unleashed a civil war killing and maiming hundreds of thousands. We have rounded up more tens of thousands of people, dragging them from their homes in the middle of the night, and throwing them into prisons. There are millions of widows, orphans, and people driven from their homes and their livelihoods. Two million Iraqis have fled the country, mostly the best educated, depriving the nation of those who would be needed to re-build it. And now our government is spying on Americans, holding foreign nationals forever without detailing any cause for doing so, and allowing no hearing, no trial. The U.S Congress is having debates on just how much the United Sates of America should torture people! We have utterly lost all pretense at having the moral high ground. People susceptible to becoming terrorists have been told for years that the U.S. is the "Great Satan". And now we behave as the Great Satan, creating terrorists far faster that we can possibly kill them.

It is clear that the fight against fanatics is not a "War" with a beginning and an end. We can not define a specific enemy. We can not even identify how many different groups of "enemies" there are, and how any of them are organized, or whether any of them are interrelated. There will be no "victory". We can not even define what would constitute a victory. It is an ongoing situation, in which we desperately need to be part of the world community, cooperating with each other, in a continuing struggle against this scourge. Ultimately the battle against terrorism can only be won through capturing the hearts and minds of people, and certainly not by brutalizing them.

The "Iraq Study Group" recommended the outlandish idea that we should even talk to people we consider "Evil". That recommendation, of course, was immediately dismissed. Have we assumed that all who disagree with us are utterly irrational? The news reports daily details of how and how many people have been killed and wounded in Iraq - but there is not one word as to who killed them or why. Who are these "terrorists" who are willing and anxious to kill themselves in order to kill innocent bystanders, and who is behind them directing their activities? Is their objective simply to cause wanton death and destruction, or is there some rationale behind their actions? How many different groups are involved, and how many of them have any connection and overall organization? Can we identify the leaders, and is there any room for negotiated settlements? It should have long ago become apparent that simply trying to kill all of the "evil doers" isn't working. Isolating Iran, Syria, and other powerful nations isn't working. We certainly have some different objectives and aims from these people, but doesn't it make sense to try to engage them in discussions to identify if there may be some common ground to work together in areas where we may not be diametrically opposed?

After the attacks of September 11, 2001 the world was united in disgust for the people who had perpetrated such a crime and in empathy with the United States. As we conducted a military campaign to drive the Taliban government out of Afghanistan and deprive Al Qaeda of a base of unfettered operations, the world was with us.

But next, rather than to concentrate on stabilizing Afghanistan, and continuing to pursue operations to root Al Qaeda from any safe haven they could find, George W. Bush announced that our real enemy was an "Axis of Evil" consisting of Iraq, Iran, and North Korea. Odd that this should be an Axis, in that Iraq and Iran were enemies who had recently concluded a ten year war, and North Korea didn't have much to do with either one. He also announced that Saddam Hussein was amassing stockpiles of "Weapons of Mass Destruction" (WMDs) and presented a "Grave and Gathering" danger to the United States and to the world. If we did not immediately demand that he abandon his program of amassing such weapons and dispose of the stockpiles he had accumulated, we would awaken to a mushroom cloud over our cities. Certainly enough to scare the bejesus out of anyone! Who would want to argue that we could ignore a threat like that! So he asked the U.S. Congress to pass a resolution demanding the Saddam get rid of the stockpiles of WMDs, and then went to the United Nations and asked for the same resolution, which they passed. But then the United Nations did something peculiar that George hadn't counted on – they wanted to verify that Saddam actually had such weapons!

The United Nations insisted that Saddam produce a list of what weapons he actually had, and an accounting of what had become of weapons he had had previously. They required that Saddam allow teams of inspectors to come look everywhere and talk to everyone who might know anything about weapons and verify what was there. George could scarcely object to what was certainly a very reasonable plan, so he said "Sure, let's send in inspectors". In the meantime, he mounted a build up of troops and materiel in preparation for an invasion. A few months later, when the build up was complete, it became obvious that he had played the United Nations, the Congress of the United States, and the people of the world for suckers. The fact that the inspectors could find no trace of any stockpiles of WMDs was in no way going to dissuade George from his planned invasion.

Other than Tony Blair, the heads of governments of every other nation on earth told George not to do it, and the British people overwhelmingly disagreed with Tony. One weekend when it was obvious that George was intent on invading Iraq, millions of people across America and around the world turned out in demonstrations to tell him not to do it. A reporter asked George what he thought of that, and his answer was: "I don't listen to them people".

And suddenly, as we began dropping bombs on Iraqi people, it was announced that "Operation Iraqi Freedom" had begun! All of a sudden it was no longer about WMDs, it was about freeing the Iraqi people from the clutches of an evil dictator, and (those that we didn't kill or maim in the process) they would thank us with chocolates and flowers. After we "freed" them, and instead of giving us chocolates and flowers, they gave us roadside improvised explosive devices and suicide bombers, and we never again heard the words "Operation Iraqi Freedom". The purpose of the war had morphed again, and it was now about building a stable democracy in the Middle East that all the surrounding nations would emulate. And we staged an "election" to show that we had created a "democracy".

Of course, one must ask, how and why did "democracy" become a goal? The ancient Greeks who invented democracy didn't think much of it. Aristotle was sure that democracy was not the best form of government. The American people, whose forefathers brought the world modern democracy, apparently don't think much of it either. Half the people eligible to vote are not even registered, and in most elections, half of those who are registered don't bother to vote. What people really want, the real goals, are Freedom, Security, and Prosperity.

Freedom and opportunity to pursue their objectives: education, vocation, and avocations; to create and invent, to form bonds and relationships; to love; and to form a family; to travel; to participate in their religious rites, rituals, and practices; and to express their opinions.

Security to know that when they and their loved ones leave the house in the morning, they will return safely in the evening; that there are people to protect their nation from outside aggression, and to protect their neighborhood and their home from crime and violence and to enforce the rule of law throughout the land; and that when disasters occur, that there are those who will fight fires, provide relief from floods, earthquakes, and windstorms, and that medical treatment is available and affordable; and that there will be a provision for them in their old age.

Prosperity both for themselves and their families, and throughout the land; that they will be able to have a nice home, food, and clothing; that fuel, electric power, water, sewers, telephones and connections for television and internet, roads, railroads, and air travel will be available and functioning properly; that they will be able to afford to pursue their hobbies, take vacations and travel; and that there will not be others in their land who are destitute, but that all will be able to partake of the bounty.

Democracy is not an objective in and of itself, but only a means to make Government responsive to the real wants, needs, and desires of the People, and to keep Government from creating self-important politicians who wish to usurp the power that has been entrusted to them, and use it to pursue personal objectives. And with an informed and free electorate, it does work – not necessarily quickly – but eventually government officials who have lost sight of the reason for their being elected do get turned out, and replaced by those who at least say they will work for the goals of the People. And those elected replace those defeated smoothly and within the laws of the land, and without chaos or coup.

But in trying to bring "democracy" to Iraq, we totally lost sight of providing any of the things that the people actually wanted. We have brought these poor people chaos, death, and destruction far worse than that they suffered under the evil dictator. We had no plan for managing post-Saddam Iraq. Instead of retaining the army, we turned the soldiers loose - hundreds of thousands of young men trained to arms, with no jobs, no incomes, and nothing to do. Instead of retaining the local and regional governments, the police, and all of the people responsible for managing the day to day affairs of the nation, we disbanded them, upset the social order, and left all of the formerly rich and powerful to organize an insurgency, using all of the disgruntled young men who had been in the army as their tools of destruction. At a fraction of the cost we are expending on military operations, we could have retained the army and put them on our payroll, and had them maintain peace and security throughout the land. We could have retained all of the local and regional governments and all the personnel employed by them, and put them all on our payroll. We could have hired hundreds of thousands of Iraqis for public works projects: rebuilding roads, bridges, power plants, water and sewer facilities, and oil pumping facilities and pipelines, and put them all on our payroll. And soon the economy would have been humming and self sustaining and we could have left. But we didn't do any of that.

But then, our purpose for being there morphed again. Shortly after our "success" of bringing "democracy" to Iraq, as the country descended into a senseless civil war, our purpose for being there was because we had to "stay the course" in order to honor our troops, that they would not have died in vain, and that we would not "suffer a defeat" that would "embolden" our enemies.

In this entire disastrous fiasco, we have alienated and lost all the respect of our friends and enemies alike. We have emasculated the United Nations, and left NATO as a shell. We are the rogue nation, more feared and disliked than those we consider to be the evil threats to the world. We went with no one's approval, and over their protestations, and I am sure that a great many people around the world are delighted to see the mess we have gotten ourselves into.

Prior to the invasion of Iraq, there was a lot of conversation about the "Pottery Barn Rule: You Break It You Own It". There was also conversation about the "Quagmire" of Viet Nam. The Bush administration scoffed at such suggestions and assured us that they had no relevance to this situation. Well, here we are so many years later, we certainly broke it, and we certainly are firmly embroiled in a quagmire. No one really knows what will happen when we leave – quite likely the immediate aftermath will be hideous. There will likely be a great deal of additional chaos, death and destruction. But while we stay, there is ongoing chaos, death and destruction. And assuming that we are not staying forever, there is no reason to believe that staying longer will make things any better when we do leave. It is time to go. And if they must, let them have their civil war. Not a good solution, but there is no good solution.

And meanwhile back at the ranch: We have "Homeland Security".

In order to scare the piss out of the populace, and get them to vote for the politicians that will "protect them", we have done some really weird things.

Continuously telling us that we are in "Code Red", are about to meet our doom, and need to be on the alert, actually has the reverse affect. How many times do they think they can "cry wolf" before we become complacent. What will they do if there is ever a situation that really requires public awareness?

Another example, Congress decided that it would somehow keep terrorists from entering the United States if every American traveling to Mexico and Canada would need a passport. So they enacted legislation to require it. But they never bothered to consider just how many millions of people who didn't have passports would suddenly need to apply for one, and whether the agency that processes applications was adequately staffed to meet that surge in demand. They weren't! And Congress had to rescind the passport requirement until a future date.

Then there is Airport Security. The great failing with security on September 11, 2001, wasn't that people were able to get on airplanes with razor knives. It was that there was a policy that if someone wanted to take over a commercial airplane, the pilot and crew should let them! The airline pilots had been asking for twenty five years prior to that time for secure cockpit doors. Except for allowing the crazies to take over the plane, a crazy with a knife, or even a gun, is no more dangerous on an airplane than they would be in any other place full of people. What passes for airport security is aimed at creating maximum inconvenience for passengers, with minimal effect on safety. Standing in long lines with my shoes and belt off and my three ounce bottles of toothpaste and aftershave tucked in a zip-lock bag, watching security people pat down an eight year old girl, and listening to announcements that we are now in "CODE ORANGE!" has made airplane travel a truly unpleasant experience. I long for the good old days when they would ask me if I had packed my own bomb, or did someone else pack it for me. The incredible army of people and incredible cost of searching for fingernail scissors would be far better spent on hiring more Beagles, or developing and deploying better technology to identify explosives.

It is enough to make me want to go home and wrap the house in plastic sheet and duct tape!

CHAPTER 25
ISRAEL

I have not had the experiences that many people living in Israel have had. I did not flee the horrors of the Nazis, only to find that no nation on earth, particularly the United States, would have me. And the only place I could go was to the Biblical land of my forefathers. I did not carve a vibrant and vital nation out of the desert. I have not fought war after war, watching family and friends die, in a struggle to hang on to that land. And perhaps if I had, the thought of leaving that land would be unthinkable.

And so, I fervently hope that what I am about to propose is utterly wrong. That the peoples of the Middle East can, in fact, learn to live along side each other in peace. But, tragically, that has yet to happen.

When The Middle East was partitioned in 1947 and Israel was created, there were some six hundred thousand Arabs who did not want to become "Israeli" and were left stateless. Living in Gaza and along the West Bank of the Jordan, they have come to be known as Palestinians. There are now six million of them. And in another sixty years there will be sixty million of them. And they will continue to hate Israel, and Israel will continue to be a catalyst for hatred and self destruction throughout the Middle East, and the crude weapons of the Middle East nations will continue to become more sophisticated and more devastating.

The position of Israel surrounded by ever growing masses of people who hate them with self-destructive passion will continue to become more and more untenable.

Although there are many who will consider it to be sacrilege, it is time to start to plan to move Israel out of the Middle East. There are dozens of pieces of real estate within the borders of the United States that are larger than the Sate of Israel, and that are currently inhabited by three men and a dog. If the United States would cede a piece of land to create a new Israel in North America, and if the world community would help to fund the move, it would go a long way toward bringing the blessings of peace to Israelis, to Americans, to Arabs, and to the world. The savings from being able to radically reduce the military expenditures by Israel and by the U.S. might give a very good economic pay back on that investment. Also, the Israelis are a very inventive and industrious people. Having them at peace and adjacent to us would create a boon of economic activity to both peoples. If a site could be found that would lie between the United States and Mexico, that would avoid having an Israel surrounded by The United States, and might have a tremendous beneficial impact on the economy of Mexico.

Of course there will be many people in both The United States and in Israel with a tremendous resistance to the concept. There will be Israelis who say: "God gave this land to my fathers, and it is mine!" But didn't God create the entire Earth, and give it all to the fathers of all of us? Do we really want to think of God as a real estate agent parceling out pieces of land, or is God the omnipotent creator of the heavens and the Earth, who has granted us the wisdom to make choices for peace? There will be those in the United States who will say: "Why should we give up our land?" And: "I don't want those people living here!" Well, we're really not talking about much land. And maybe by the time this becomes a reality, the bigots will have died off, and been replaced by their children, who are accepting of all peoples, and who long for World Peace. It will take a long time to overcome the resistance. And it will take a long time to solve the very real problems involved in moving a nation of six million people.

Actually, most of the current older adult population of Israel may never make the move. It will require years of talking and arguing about the merits before anyone actually takes the concept of moving seriously. And it will require many more years of looking at various sites, formulating plans, securing pledges for financing, and actually passing resolutions by both governments to authorize it. I would estimate that in today dollars, the cost of rebuilding an Israel in North America - roads, power, water, sewers, public buildings, homes, factories, farms, etc. and moving people, possessions, and equipment - will be approximately one trillion dollars. Although that sounds like a lot of money, it would not all be required nor all be spent at one time, but over a period of many years. We will likely spend that much money in the invasion and occupation of Iraq, and as a means of promoting peace in the Middle East and in the world, we're not likely to have anything to show for it.

Once a site is established and moving is authorized, it will require years of mapping and planning before the first shovelful of earth is turned. The first to move then, would be people in the construction industry – construction would be accomplished by some combination of Israeli and American crews – building the roads and infrastructure. This will be an enormous boon to American workers in the construction trades. Completing construction and moving will require many more years. Starting from today, the soonest this could become a reality, and be completed, is probably twenty five to thirty years. The population that will actually be the beneficiaries will be the children, and children who have not yet been conceived.

Unfortunately, we have become a nation of people looking for instant gratification. As with many of the proposals made in this book, this one would require planning, monetary expenditure, hard work, and self-sacrifice by people living today, to achieve blessings to the generations to follow. And we have shown a great reluctance to pursue such courses of action. But what would we have today, if Americans in 1776 were unwilling to "pledge their lives, their fortunes, and their sacred honor" for the benefit of our generation living more than two hundred years later?

EPILOGUE

Thank you for reading my book.

I hope that you found it reasonably entertaining. Whether you found the opinions expressed to be good, bad, aggravating, disgusting, or incredibly stupid, so long as you didn't find them boring, I have accomplished my task.

I can only hope that this book may have provoked some thought, and perhaps some discussion, on the topics presented.

Many of the problems discussed are easy to ignore. They are long term problems. There is no catastrophic event to force us to sit up and take notice, to catapult us into action. Tomorrow the world population will only be two hundred fifty thousand more people than today, and we really won't notice. Tomorrow we will only have burned up another eighty million barrels of the planet's remaining petroleum, and we won't really feel that we are any closer to the time when there will be no more. And in burning that petroleum, we will dump a few more tons of pollutants into our atmosphere, but the sun will still rise, and we won't notice a difference. Our National debt will grow by a few hundred million dollars, but nothing will feel different. But the cumulative effect of continuing to ignore these situations day after day after day eventually will create catastrophe, and then it will be too late to fix them.

Mainly, I hope that I have helped to create an atmosphere where those who serve in our governments, and those who aspire to serve, will be held accountable for dealing with real issues, and for presenting clear proposals for dealing with those issues.

And that those in the news media will be held accountable for asking real questions and insisting on real answers, and for reporting in depth the positions they force those public servants and aspiring public servants to enunciate. That they will not be satisfied with sound bites, or reporting on how people looked or sounded or what they wore, or how many places they have appeared, or the results of polls reporting how many people like them or dislike them – people like you, who haven't been given enough real information to form the basis on which to make an intelligent opinion.